From
SACRIFICE
to
CELEBRATION

A Lenten Journey

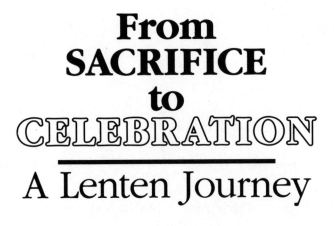

From
SACRIFICE
to
CELEBRATION

A Lenten Journey

by Evan Drake Howard

Judson Press ® Valley Forge

From Sacrifice to Celebration: A Lenten Journey

© 1993 by Evan Drake Howard
Published by Judson Press, Valley Forge, PA 19482-0851

Unless otherwise indicated, Bible quotations in this volume are from the New Revised Standard Version of the Bible, copyrighted 1989 by the Division of Christian Education of the National Council of the Churches of Christ in the United States of America, and are used by permission. All rights reserved. Other quotations are from *The Holy Bible*, King James Version, and the Revised Standard Version of the Bible, copyrighted © 1946, 1952, 1971, by the division of Christian Education of the National Council of the Churches of Christ in the U.S. A., and used by permission. All rights reserved.

Library of Congress Cataloging-in-Publication Data

Howard, Evan Drake, 1955-
From sacrifice to celebration: a Lenten journey/by Evan Drake Howard.
    p. cm.
Includes bibliographical references.
ISBN 0-8170-1197-8
1. Lent—Prayer-books and devotions—English. I. Title
BV85.H6837 1993
242'.34—dc20   93-22693

Printed in the U.S.A.

*With thanksgiving
for the people of
Central Baptist Church,
Providence, Rhode Island*

Contents

Foreword

by Gilbert Bilezikian

As you get into this book, it begins pulsing in your hands with a life of its own. And well it should, since it probes the mysteries of life and death at the intersection of human destiny and divine love. As it registers the awesome journey of the Savior to the cross and on to resurrection glory, the book resonates with the life-giving love of God reaching down to human beings through the shadows of death to lead them into the sunburst of life reclaimed.

The cross is obviously constructed of two sections: the vertical shaft and the crossbeam. One without the other does not constitute a cross. In his letter to the Philippians, Paul mentioned people who lived as enemies of the cross. Unfortunately, even God-fearing, well-meaning Christians can act as enemies of the cross without ever knowing it; they endeavor to separate its two segments and reduce it to only one of its elements.

The vertical trunk of the cross represents our relationship with God. By sending the Savior from above to reach down and save us in the depths of our need, God initiated reconciliation with us. Christ's death gives us access to the divine love of God.

The horizontal beam of the cross represents our gathering in community. The Savior's hands were nailed to this section in a posture that shows his outstretched arms embracing all those who seek reconciliation with God and thereby with one another.

Jesus reduced the totality of the Christian faith to two great commandments that summarized the Law and the prophets:

Love God and love your neighbor as yourself. This is the cross. Our love for God is the vertical relationship; our love for others is the horizontal one. There is no genuine Christianity without the two. Our identity as believers is to be found at the intersection of the two segments of the cross: love for God and love for others.

Unfortunately, Christians tend to be polarizers of the cross. Some reduce Christianity to a personal relationship with God. Having received Christ as their Savior, they apply themselves to the cultivation of the vertical dimension of their faith. They assiduously pursue spiritual disciplines and rarely miss the practice of their devotional exercises. However, as absorbed as they are in their personal piety, they have no time or concern for the needs of others and for the plight of a tormented world. Like the priest and the Levite in Jesus' parable, they travel the road of life seeing the tragic needs all around them but refusing to do anything to relieve them.

Other Christians unduly minimize the importance of an individual relationship with God and devote themselves to social causes such as the rescue of the hungry, the poor, and the oppressed. They fulfill the second great commandment but neglect the first. They affirm the horizontal dimension of the cross, but they kick away its support.

This book brilliantly avoids dismembering the cross either way. It honors the cross by leaving it intact. Much of the author's journey to mature faith is reflected in these pages. As the reader ponders them, each page will scintillate with fresh insights that illumine, nourish, inspire, and motivate. I commend the reader for obtaining this book and for the enrichment it will bring to her or his life. But mostly, as a longtime friend of the author and his theologian-teammate, Carol, I commend him for having poured his noble soul into this writing and for having thus made a signal contribution to our growth in the love of God and in the love for our human community.

— *Gilbert Bilezikian*
Wheaton College
Wheaton, Illinois

Acknowledgments

Writing a book is a journey, as is the movement through Lent to Easter. I am grateful for the companions who traveled the way with me and gave their support.

Mary Nicol of Judson Press first encouraged me to undertake this project as a sequel to my Advent book, *Rekindling the Hope of the Manger*. I am thankful for her consistent optimism and honest but gentle feedback from start to finish.

Kathleen Hayes, also at Judson, offered helpful comments early on and later lent her editorial skill to producing the completed manuscript.

I thank my wife, Carol, for suggesting the title, and our friend Gilbert Bilezikian for writing the foreword.

I am also grateful to the people of my congregation, Central Baptist Church of Providence, Rhode Island, for graciously receiving my ideas about Lent and Easter in sermons and group studies.

Introduction

"I'm bored to tears!" The words come to our lips when there's nothing good on TV. They reverberate in our minds when we are working longer hours and enjoying the job less. They simmer in our hearts when we are sitting in a traffic jam or ransacking the video store to find a movie we haven't seen yet.

Boredom. It's the curse of our times! The age of instant information, push-button conveniences, and high-tech entertainment has created such short attention spans that psychic numbness sets in if we miss our daily fix of a thrill a minute.

In *The Great Gatsby*, F. Scott Fitzgerald's parable of modern life, Daisy asks, "What'll we do with ourselves this afternoon? . . . and the day after that, and the next thirty years?"

Good question. As a pastor, I hear the question a lot. If not spoken directly, it is communicated in the furrowed brows and anxious body language of my parishioners. Many are asking, How can I rise above the humdrum predictability of my life? If I'm so busy, why do I feel so barren? How can I keep my sanity when my lifestyle is such a treadmill?

I wrote this book because I have found in Lent the hope of deliverance. Lent is a season for these times. It does not pander to us with quick fixes or self-help platitudes; it refuses to allow us the comforts of our dishonesties or the false security of our evasions. Lent calls us to discipline. At its best, Lent is more than a season; it's a journey from the daily grind to spiritual growth.

Realism is the watchword of Lent. Rooted in Jesus' time of trial in the wilderness, these forty days speak powerfully to people who find themselves in wildernesses of emotional or relational brokenness, as many do today. Apart from being desolate and dangerous, the wilderness is deathly boring. It is the place of loneliness, self-doubt, and temptation. People who sojourn there must rely on faith and grace to see them through.

That's what Jesus did, and the lessons he learned in the wilderness informed the rest of his life. His forty days of testing solidified his relationship with God. I don't understand this mystery; I can only observe that he left the wilderness a fully integrated person, a man ready to begin a three-year ministry that would change the world.

I think Jesus experienced in the wilderness what can be described in contemporary language as "spiritual bonding." Bonding is the forming of an intimate tie that enhances the meaning of the lives involved. Jesus underwent this process in a spiritual sense. He invites us to do the same.

The result of Jesus' bonding with God was the complete surrender of his will to God's will. This surrender empowered him in ministry and enabled him to accept the challenge of the cross; it made his time in this world anything but ordinary. Having bonded with God in the wilderness, and having discovered that God's grace is always sufficient, Jesus emerged ready to face anything. What he faced, first of all, were relationships with a wide variety of people. We will meet some of them in the following chapters; their stories are told in readings from the Gospels selected from the lectionary of the Christian year. Following these stories will take us from the first Sunday in Lent to Easter Sunday.

The people you will meet in the Gospel lessons have something in common: In the midst of their inner wilderness experiences, they broke boredom's curse by forming the same spiritual bond with Jesus that he had formed with God. This bonding freed them from dead routine and brought them new life.

Whether you use this book on your personal journey through Lent to Easter, or study it in a group, I hope you will see yourself in the people you meet here. They are as ordinary as you or me, but the wonder of the gospel story is that God's grace came to them in Jesus Christ and made their lives extraordinary. May that same grace be yours as you join me on the adventure that awaits.

1

Beyond the Boredom Syndrome

A Reading from the Gospel According to Luke (4:1-13)
Jesus, full of the Holy Spirit, returned from the Jordan and was led by the Spirit in the wilderness, where for forty days he was tempted by the devil. He ate nothing at all during those days, and when they were over, he was famished. The devil said to him, "If you are the Son of God, command this stone to become a loaf of bread." Jesus answered him, "It is written, 'One does not live by bread alone.' "

Then the devil led him up and showed him in an instant all the kingdoms of the world. And the devil said to him, "To you I will give their glory and all this authority; for it has been given over to me, and I give it to anyone I please. If you, then, will worship me, it will all be yours." Jesus answered him, "It is written, 'Worship the Lord your God, and serve only him.' "

Then the devil took him to Jerusalem, and placed him on the pinnacle of the temple, saying to him, "If you are the Son of God, throw yourself down from here, for it is written, 'He will command his angels concerning you, to protect you,' and 'On their hands they will bear you up, so that you will not dash your foot against a stone.' " Jesus answered him, "It is said, 'Do not put the Lord your God to the test.' " When the devil had finished every test, he departed from him until an opportune time.

I confess. I struggle with the somber tone of Lent. The holy birth at Christmas, the Resurrection at Easter, the descent of the

1

Spirit at Pentecost—these I welcome and celebrate with joy. But from Ash Wednesday to Good Friday, as the mood shifts from celebration to contemplation, from exuberant praise to reverent introspection, my spirit rebels.

The Lenten traditions of repentance and self-sacrifice can make these forty days seem like drudgery. When that happens, the possibility of renewal fades, and I begin longing for an easier path to spiritual enrichment. This is why I need a reminder each year that Lent is not about drudgery; it's about drama—the drama of bonding with Christ on the Calvary road toward an encounter with God. From this broader perspective, Lent is more than seriousness and solemnity. Like faith itself, it's an adventure beyond the ordinary.

The Dangers of Dullness

One thing about adventure—it's never boring. Once boredom sets in, adventure ends. Bored people go through meaningless motions; they get trapped in dead routines, frozen in stagnant rituals. Wherever boredom intrudes, whether into a career or a friendship, a learning endeavor or a recreational activity, it brings disillusionment. And when boredom creeps into the life of faith, it weakens commitment and stymies joy. That's why I need a season of Lent. When my journey of faith seems stuck in the ruts of indifference or predictability, Lent propels me forward again. Lent has the power to move us beyond the boredom syndrome. But this happens only when we discover that bonding more deeply with Christ is life's greatest adventure. Apart from a vital experience of his grace, we become targets of boredom's subtle but devastating effects.

Consider, for instance, the warning sounded by Alan Caruba, a creative humorist and social commentator. Caruba has made a name for himself by identifying the link between boredom and many of today's haunting problems. He contends that we can trace everything from drug and alcohol abuse to divorce and suicide to boredom's destructive influence. Research shows that 80 percent of the inmates in U.S. prisons say they were bored with school. Finding nothing to interest them in their studies, many of them dropped out and got in with the wrong crowd.

Eventually they ended up in a life of crime and found themselves behind bars, at a high cost to themselves and society.

Boredom causes loneliness. It leads to the breakup of relationships simply because they have lost their spark. In today's mobile society, people respond to boredom by moving from one job to another, or one place to another, in a never-ending search for a more stimulating environment. In the process, they sacrifice familiarity and intimacy. Having lost their roots, they feel assaulted by a cosmic sense of aloneness.

Marriages end when husbands and wives get bored with each other (more on this later). Addictions begin when people try to escape life's tedium through substances such as drugs, alcohol, and food, or processes such as gambling or shopping, television watching or sexual fantasizing. Serial marriages and artificial ecstasy prescribed as remedies for life's monotony only leave people empty and broken.[1]

As a pastor, I am particularly aware of how rampant boredom is among Christians. During a children's sermon once, I was naive enough to ask the boys and girls of my congregation how they felt about being in church on Sunday morning. A five-year-old raised his hand and shouted, ''It's boring!''

I know some adults who would agree with that little boy's opinion. They seldom attend worship. They rarely pray, study the Bible, or form nurturing relationships with other believers. And they *never* become involved in ministries of service or mission. Although many of these people are Christians who grew up in the church, they have become captives of the boredom syndrome. Their faith has lost its vigor; their spiritual lives are stuck in neutral.

Thank God for Lent! Lent is a time for new beginnings, a time for rediscovering the Christian faith as the great adventure God intends it to be. The spirit of the season reminds me of a comment by Thor Heyerdahl, Norway's most famous modern-day adventurer. He gained international recognition for his sea travels aboard the Sumerian-style balsa raft he built called Kon Tiki. As he sailed Kon Tiki from Peru to Polynesia to prove a point about ancient migration patterns, he observed that the real dangers on such an adventure lie not out at sea but close to shore. Near the shore a boat can run aground on a sandbar or shallow reef; it can get dashed against the rocks or swamped by the pounding surf. On the open sea there are no such dangers, only the freedom of the wind and the mystery of the deep.

So it is with faith. The closer we stay to the familiar coastline of our present spiritual awareness, the more likely we are to run aground on the rocky shoals of boredom. Bonding intimately with Christ on a Lenten adventure beyond the ordinary prevents this disaster. The work of the Holy Spirit makes this bonding possible, inviting us out of the safe but stifling harbors of complacency onto the high seas of enlivened faith.

During Lent, the Christ who was obedient to God's call summons us to similar obedience. Before he began his ministry, his faith led him into the wilderness, where he was tempted by the devil. Whenever we try to move beyond the boredom syndrome, we too will meet opposition in the form of temptation.

A Miracle Best Left Undone

In his inner spirit Jesus hears the devil say, "If you are the Son of God, command this stone to become a loaf of bread" (Luke 4:3). Commentators have traditionally emphasized the physical nature of the first temptation. The devil tries to get Jesus to satisfy his hunger rather than trust in God for sustenance. If Jesus would feed not only himself but also the masses, he would win popular acclaim by giving people material bread, not the better spiritual food of his liberating message. Satan hopes that Jesus will put his physical needs above his spiritual allegiance and, performing a miracle under his own power, make an idol of his success. Such misguided priorities would have deterred Jesus from preaching the kingdom of God and thwarted his mission to the cross.

Recognizing the psychological overtones of this physical temptation casts the matter in contemporary terms. Like Jesus, modern people are tempted every day to value their performance more than their personhood, to sacrifice who they are in order to win approval for what they do. The result of this emphasis on proving our worth is a tendency to define ourselves outwardly by success rather than inwardly by character.

Such psychological assaults exploit the vulnerability of a person's ego. The Adversary knows that the human need for recognition and affirmation runs so deep that many of us never learn the higher art of accepting ourselves as God accepts us. Instead, we try to earn acceptance by looking good or acting suave, by marrying well or making more, by giving until it hurts or working until we drop. The taunt to "turn those stones to bread" that Satan directed toward Jesus in the wilderness reverberates in our psyches whenever we try to be more or do more to win someone's approval.

Having wrongly ordered priorities is the human tendency, and disobedience to God soon results. Being overly impressed with our own gifts and skills comes naturally to many of us. Subtle though such conceit may be, it produces a swelled head and an insatiable need for 'strokes' from others. We become trapped in a condition of dependency, exchanging the adventure of faith for the stagnation of the wilderness. In this dependent condition, the salt of the Christian life loses its savor, and a drift toward boredom begins. Caught in monotony's undertow, believers become prideful yet insecure cynics rather than transformed people who bring hope to the world.

Coach Don Shula of the Miami Dolphins found himself humiliated by the "ego trap" while on vacation in Maine. He and his wife had gone there to escape the pressures of the limelight in Florida, where he can't even go shopping without drawing a crowd. When the Shulas arrived in a secluded Maine town, they encountered rainy weather, so they decided to go to a movie. Upon walking into the lighted theater, they were greeted by the applause of the small audience gathered there. As they sat down, Shula whispered to his wife, "I guess there's no place where I'm not known." When a man from the audience came over to shake his hand, Shula said, "I'm surprised you know me!" To which the man replied, "Do I know you? We just applauded because we're glad to see you folks. The manager wouldn't start the film until at least ten people came in."[2]

Snared by the ego trap, we may seem outwardly gracious, but we are inwardly discontent and wrongly motivated if self-interest, not God, reigns in our hearts. When this happens we don't see others as equals but as rivals. We are interested in them not because we find joy in sharing their lives but because we need them to help us feel good about ourselves.

Jesus withstood this temptation by drawing on a spiritual insight: "One does not live by bread alone, but by every word that comes from the mouth of God" (Matthew 4:4). He knew that success cannot produce inner integration, that its rewards, though scintillating, are as fleeting as evening shadows. These rewards may bring recognition, wealth, and popularity, but apart from God's presence, the words of British author John Masefield hold true: "Success is the brand on the brow of the man who has aimed too low." Jesus challenges us to aim higher, as high as the Word that comes from the mouth of God. That Word, embodied first in Scripture and then in Christ's own person, is the bread of heaven, and whoever eats of this bread shall live.

Lent is a time for feeding on God's Word. It's a time for nourishing our spirits on the good news of our acceptance in Christ. Fed and nourished, we transcend our aloneness and find community with others. We discover that our highest purpose is to do God's will, as Jesus did. Captivated by this purpose, we leave the boredom of the wilderness behind and bond with the Savior on his adventure of faith to the cross. Fasting from our preoccupation with success—from trying to turn stones into bread on our own power—we begin to feast on the wonder and joy of God's presence. As this presence convicts, converts, and consecrates our hearts, we find the truth that sets us free.

The Politics of Having It All

Next, Jesus envisions the Tempter showing him in an instant all the kingdoms of the world and saying, "To you I will give their glory and all this authority; for it has been given over to me, and I give it to anyone I please. If you, then, will worship me, it will all be yours" (Luke 4:6-7).

The second temptation is political, though it also has psychological overtones. Satan offers Jesus the chance to rule the world. Sound nice? With that kind of authority, he could have it all—adulation without achievement, wealth without work, pleasure without restriction.

Who wouldn't be tempted by such an offer? The German philosopher Friedrich Nietzsche believed we all would. He argued that "the will to power" governs our loyalties; so did Alfred Adler, one of the fathers of modern psychology. The will to power is our need to be in control, to have the rest of the world revolve around us. This need affects all our relationships, whether in the home, the workplace, or the halls of national or international politics.

If left unregulated and undisciplined, the will to power gives rise to what Steven Berglas of Harvard Medical School calls 'pathological narcissism.' In a *Time* magazine interview, he emphasized that this preoccupation with self makes the pursuit of power inevitable but the management of it impossible. Self-absorbed people become susceptible to what Berglas calls "the four *A's*—arrogance, a sense of aloneness, the need to seek adventure, and adultery."

Narcissists seek one new conquest after another but never find fulfillment. Pete Rose, Gary Hart, Imelda Marcos, Jimmy Swaggart, Jim Bakker, Ivan Boesky, Michael Milken—all of them tasted brokenness because of their pathological need for power, whether financial, political, or religious. They tried to fill the empty void within with the counterfeit esteem garnered from the rewards of their drivenness.[3]

Other disturbing news stories also highlight the problem of power-seeking. On the heels of the confrontation between Anita Hill and Supreme Court Justice Clarence Thomas, nationwide concerns surfaced about sexual harassment, which experts say is not as much about sex as about power. The rivalry between the United States and Japan, the smoldering racial hostilities in urban America, and the ongoing battle over abortion—aren't these struggles also fundamentally about power?

The same desire for domination that creates conflict between groups wreaks havoc in each human heart. Our heart's vulnerability to this ancient nemesis inspired Lord Acton's insight that "power corrupts and absolute power corrupts absolutely." The seeds of corruption are rooted in human pride. When asked what's wrong with the world, G. K. Chesterton touched the heart of the matter with his answer: "I am!"

The will to power can bring out the worst in people. It leads politicians to wage negative campaigns, drives business people to adopt cutthroat sales tactics, and engages parents and children in battles for supremacy in the home. The hunger for power can incite sentiments bordering on the ridiculous, as evidenced in the words of William Howard Taft's great-grand-

daughter. In her third-grade autobiography, she wrote, "My
great-grandfather was President of the United States, my grandfather was a United States senator, my father is an ambassador,
and I am a Brownie."

Ridiculous is also how the devil wants Jesus to look in the
wilderness. In the second temptation, Satan invites Jesus to sell
his soul, like Goethe's Faust, for the chance to "have it all." But
Jesus refuses to give up his adventure of faith for such a superficial prize as that. It is as if he hears the anguish of the hungry,
the moans of the sick, the cries of the oppressed, and commits
himself to help them instead. He knows that without God, "having it all" is not heaven but hell. If he would sell his soul to the
devil by bowing down to worship him, he might gain the whole
world; but that world would be deathly boring because God
would not be in it.

I wonder if Jesus, in the face of the second temptation, looked
into the future and saw the world of today. If he did, and if this
world is what the devil offered him, he rejected the offer for
good reason: Today's world has rejected God and become a boring wilderness as a result. Without God, everything degenerates
into meaninglessness and monotony. Television becomes boring.
So do books and movies, music and the arts. Even passionate activities such as learning and sports and sex are boring if God is
not in them to reveal their higher purpose. Knowing this, Jesus
says no to the devil's offer. He resists the temptation to gain the
whole world but lose his own soul. Jesus did not come to be a
political ruler; he came to be a suffering Savior. His kingdom is
not of this world. His kingdom is a heavenly kingdom, estab-
lished in the hearts of his people in time, revealed in power and
glory in eternity.

From Addiction to Surrender

At this point the devil resorts to desperate tactics. He seems
to say to himself, "I have tried to ruin this man physically and
politically, but it hasn't worked; I'll have to change my
strategy." So in Jesus' mind Satan takes him to Jerusalem, places
him on the pinnacle of the temple, and says, "If you are the Son
of God, throw yourself down from here" (Luke 4:9).

This third temptation is spiritual. The devil tries to get Jesus to test God. He wants Jesus to risk his bodily health by performing a spectacular but suicidal stunt to see if God will intervene to save him. During Lent, we acknowledge the ways we are similarly tempted. Lent is the season for affirming the oneness of body and soul in the Christian life. It's also the season for renewing our commitment to care for both.

Christianity has been called the most materialistic of the world's major religions. This is because the eternal Spirit became one with mortal flesh in Jesus Christ. In the Incarnation, God elevated ordinary matter, Eden's dust, to a position of new dignity. The Scriptures teach that the body is the temple of the Holy Spirit and that there will be a continuity between our physical body in this world and our spiritual body in the next.

Though we do not understand this mystery, we know it has implications for how we treat what God has created. Redemption in Christ is physical as well as spiritual, social as well as personal. Lent reminds us of this wholistic emphasis. It is the season for getting honest about the ways we test God by abusing our bodies and expecting divine deliverance. Tobacco and caffeine, sweets and preservatives, rich foods and late nights, too much alcohol and too little exercise—who among us is not susceptible to overindulging in these vices?

As Jesus was tempted to destroy himself by falling from the pinnacle of the temple, so we are tempted to sabotage our health by falling into various addictions. When boredom sets in, we turn to compulsive smoking or drinking, overeating or drug-taking, overworking or thrill-seeking to try to fill unmet spiritual needs. Such attempts to escape life's dullness can lead us to test God. It never works. Instead, testing God gets us trapped in the misery of deadly substances and destructive habits.

Disciplining our will and desires is a spiritual matter with physical implications. In the United States, the seductions of countless advertisers make discipline difficult. The excesses of commercialism invite us to live beyond our limits, increasing our vulnerability to addiction. The way to freedom is found in reorienting one's will and desire toward God. In the words of John of the Cross, "It is not the things of this world that either occupy the soul or cause it harm, since they enter it not, but rather the will and desire for them."[4]

One of Scotland's distinguished ministers of the nineteenth century, Thomas Chalmers, was riding one day behind the driver of a pony cart. At a certain point in the road, the driver drew his whip and flicked the pony sharply with it. When Dr. Chalmers protested, the driver replied, "Do you see that white post? This pony has a way of shying toward it, so when we approach it, I get his attention with a touch of the whip. That gives him something else to think about!" This experience inspired one of Chalmers's outstanding sermons, "The Expulsive Power of a New Affection," which emphasized how God helps us overcome temptation by giving us something better to think about.[5]

This is the genius of Lent. By raising our moral vision as high as the cross of Christ, Lent confronts us with our shortcomings and challenges us to overcome them. Meditating on the cross, we encounter Jesus' example of absolute surrender, his disciplined faith and radical obedience. Such surrender thwarts temptation's power. It replaces one's desire for harmful substances and lifestyles with a deeper yearning for spiritual wholeness. The cross dramatizes this yearning. It is the "something better" that God gives us to think about when temptation strikes.

The longstanding tradition of fasting or giving up harmful attitudes or actions during this season is meant to increase our discipline. Self-denial is an exercise in letting go; it is the practice of subduing the lusts of our fallen human nature by the power of the Spirit. When accompanied by new levels of internal surrender, such external sacrifice advances one's growth in grace. But it cannot be done alone; God's help is necessary. Just as our fasting will falter unless spiritually empowered, so our attempt to live as Christians will fail unless divinely guided.

We cannot accomplish some goals without maximum commitment. Growth in the Christian life is one of them. Lent declares that commitment without reliance on God is futile. Attempts to resist a temptation, conquer an addiction, or grow spiritually fail without such reliance. These attempts succeed only when the self is freed from attachment.

Once you stop wanting what you do not have and loosen your grip on what you do have, you are ready to receive God's presence in a new and empowering way. Filled with this presence, your restlessness will cease. You will take the less-traveled road from boredom to bonding, not the congested expressway from boredom to brokenness. On your journey, you will find adventure, the unfolding drama of life's richness.

The following chapters are about people in the Gospels who took this journey. Among them are Nicodemus, the woman of Samaria, a blind man, and the prodigal son. All of them confronted boredom in their own way, whether in religion or marriage, physical disability or family tedium. Their stories intersect with the story of Jesus, the greatest spiritual adventurer of all—and their experiences often reflect our own. As we live the forty days of adventure from Lent to Easter with them, they have much to teach us about the journey from sacrifice to celebration.

Prayer for the First Sunday in Lent

Out of my darkness and into your light,
    out of my weakness and into your strength,
        out of my poverty and into your abundance,
I come, O God, to you.

On my Lenten journey I seek a faith that is
            more than words,
                more than good intentions,
            a faith that leads me not into temptation
            but delivers me from the evil one.

I give thanks that,
            because of your grace in Jesus Christ,
            you look beyond all that is
            fallen and
                fallible and
                    flawed in me,
            and see my potential instead.

You continually call me beyond myself.

You call me beyond denial to repentance,
                beyond self-indulgence to sharing,
                beyond complacency to action.

You challenge me to leave behind my inhibitions and fears,
        that I might walk in the freedom of your Spirit.

In spite of how ordinary I am,
       I thank you for embracing me as your child,
       for making me feel special,
       an invited guest at the banqueting
       table of your love.

I live these forty days in expectation, O God of Hope.

I want to see Jesus, "who for a little while
       was made lower than the angels, now crowned with
       glory and honor because of the suffering of death,
       so that by the grace of God he might taste death
       for everyone."

Enter into the wilderness experiences of my life,
       I pray.

Remind me that he was tempted in every way as I am,
       yet without sin.

In bonding with him as he has bonded with me,
       let me hear your Word anew.

Let that Word soften the hard places within me,
         deepen the shallow places,
           fill the empty places,
       that I may not be rich in things,
       but rich in faith, eagerly awaiting
       Easter's dawn. Amen.

Questions for Reflection and Study

1. Put yourself in Jesus' place in the wilderness. Reflect on where you are most vulnerable to temptation in your own life. Being as honest as you can be, write down some of your greatest temptations. (If you are doing this in a group, the leader can collect the *unsigned* papers and read aloud what each person has written.) Reflect on the similarities and differences between Jesus' temptations and ours today. What kind of process might be involved in causing a person to fall to the most frequently mentioned temptations that were read? What might be some of the results of such a fall?

2. Why do you think Jesus was led into the wilderness to be tempted right at the beginning of his ministry? What does this say about the role of temptation in the life of faith? Why does Luke emphasize the Spirit's role in leading Jesus into the wilderness?

3. How big a role does boredom play in temptation? Do you agree or disagree that it was a factor in Jesus' experience?

4. This chapter makes the point that Jesus was tempted physically, politically, and spiritually, and that his personal psyche was involved each time. Is this a biblical paradigm for how temptation works? Or is this just one example of a complex phenomenon? Are you most easily led astray by temptations to worldly success, to power, or to testing God by indulging your addictions?

5. This chapter suggests that the temptations did not happen literally but in Jesus' mind and spirit. Why is it important to emphasize the spiritual element here and correct any tendencies toward literalism?

6. How might your understanding of Satan affect how you handle temptation in the Christian life? Is Satan always the instigator of temptation, or can it come from other sources?

7. Read Hebrews 2:14-18. If Jesus had succumbed to temptation, could he still have been the Christ? How is his experience an encouragement to you as you seek to live as a Christian?

8. What resources or personal disciplines do you find most helpful in resisting temptation? How can Lent be a time for drawing upon or practicing these with greater effectiveness?

9. How does the story of Moses and the Israelites wandering in the wilderness for forty years relate to Jesus' time of testing in Luke 4? Read 1 Corinthians 10:1-13 as background for your answer.

Notes

[1]Kay Quick, "Boring Institute Fans Should Get into the Habit of Fine Reading," *Monroe Guardian* (August 26, 1991), 4A.

[2]King Duncan, *Mule Eggs and Topknots* (Knoxville: Seven Worlds Press, 1987), 64.

[3]"The Bigger They Are, the Harder They Fall," *Time* (November 4, 1991), 14-16.

[4]Quoted in Gerald G. May, *Addiction and Grace* (San Francisco: Harper and Row, 1988), 18.

[5]Quoted in Ralph W. Sockman, *How to Believe* (Garden City, N.Y.: Doubleday & Company, Inc., 1953), 36.

2

An Invitation to Discovery

A Reading from the Gospel According to John (3:1-17)

Now there was a Pharisee named Nicodemus, a leader of the Jews. He came to Jesus by night and said to him, "Rabbi, we know that you are a teacher who has come from God; for no one can do these signs that you do apart from the presence of God." Jesus answered him, "Very truly, I tell you, no one can see the kingdom of God without being born from above." Nicodemus said to him, "How can anyone be born after having grown old? Can one enter a second time into the mother's womb and be born?" Jesus answered, "Very truly, I tell you, no one can enter the kingdom of God without being born of water and Spirit. What is born of the flesh is flesh, and what is born of the Spirit is spirit. Do not be astonished that I said to you, 'You must be born from above.' The wind blows where it chooses, and you hear the sound of it, but you do not know where it comes from or where it goes. So it is with everyone who is born of the Spirit." Nicodemus said to him, "How can these things be?" Jesus answered him, "Are you a teacher of Israel, and yet you do not understand these things?

"Very truly, I tell you, we speak of what we know and testify to what we have seen; yet you do not receive our testimony. If I have told you about earthly things and you do not believe, how can you believe if I tell you about heavenly things? No one has ascended into heaven except the one who descended from heaven, the Son of Man. And just as Moses lifted up the serpent in the wilderness, so must the Son of Man be lifted up, that whoever believes in him may have eternal life.

"For God so loved the world that he gave his only Son, so that everyone who believes in him may not perish but may have eternal life. Indeed, God did not send the Son into the world to condemn the world, but in order that the world might be saved through him."

If I were asked to name a secular movie in which Lent's call to renewed discipline can be heard, I would name *Dead Poets Society*. The year is 1959. A new teacher, Mr. Keating (played by Robin Williams), has come to the prestigious boarding school for boys, Welton Academy, from the Chester School in London, to teach English. A graduate of Welton himself, Mr. Keating has a problem: He rejects the educational philosophy of the headmaster, Dean Noland.

Mr. Keating wants to teach his students not *what* to think, as Dean Noland commands, but *how* to think for themselves. This conflict, and Mr. Keating's influence on the teenage boys who form a secret club called "The Dead Poets Society," illuminate the movie's message: Be true to yourself. In his relationship with the boys, Mr. Keating emphasizes character formation and nonconformity in light of the inevitability of death—an emphasis also of Lent.

An early scene in the movie is especially dramatic. Mr. Keating takes his poetry class out to the foyer, where pictures of students from seventy-five years ago hang on the wall. He calls on a student to read from poet Robert Herrick: "Gather ye rosebuds while ye may, / Old Time is still a-flying: / And this same flower that smiles to-day / Tomorrow will be dying." Reminding the class that their predecessors all died, and so will they, he then instructs them to lean their ears close to the pictures of the former students and hear what they say. As they listen, he whispers, as if from the grave, "*Carpe diem, carpe diem,*" which in Latin means, "Seize the day, seize the day." He urges them not to sacrifice their boyhood dreams in pursuit of fleeting pleasures, but to make their lives extraordinary.

Hope for the Hungering Heart

Mr. Keating's advice is relevant for Christians who want to make the most of Lent. The days before Easter call us back to basics. They invite reflection on the essence of what following Christ means. As we "seize" each day by meditating on Scripture and practicing the disciplines of self-examination and prayer, opportunity beckons. It is the opportunity to move from lethargy to risk, from detachment to involvement. It is the opportunity for spiritual renewal. This means that no matter how young or old we are, no matter how satisfied or needy, how broken or whole, abundant life can be ours.

It begins with awakened faith. No other kind will do. Abundant life cannot arise from faith that has drifted into the slumber of irrelevance. Yet this can easily happen. If God seems detached and distant, a vague religious concept rather than a living presence, perhaps you have been lulled into a perilous spiritual apathy. When faith's expression is reduced to a once-a-week appearance at church, it loses its power. When no longer a daily discipline of attention to God and service to others, faith degenerates into indifference.

Having experienced the freedom of forgiveness and new life in Christ, one does not become immune to the dangers of dead religion. Because of the attractions of the world, the seductions of the fallen self, or just plain inertia, authentic Christian faith can lose its growing edge.

But Lent comes to say to Christians who are externally busy without being internally fulfilled, "Slow down and examine your priorities." To those carrying heavy burdens, Lent says, "Let God share the weight, as Jesus did." Most of all, to those languishing in the grip of the ordinary, to those trapped in boredom's stranglehold, Lent offers release. It declares that life can become extraordinary when infused by the spiritual passion that led Jesus to the cross.

Nicodemus, a Pharisee and member of the Sanhedrin, came to Jesus in search of this extraordinary life. Night had fallen, and the crowds had all gone away. Apparently he had been watching Jesus from a distance, captivated by the undeniable evidences of God's power working through him.

Had Nicodemus been present when Jesus made the lame walk,

the deaf hear, and the blind see? This is implied by his reference
to Jesus' "miraculous signs" (John 3:2). Now he comes under
the cover of darkness, protecting his reputation, to seek a personal consultation. He wants to learn more about this man who
has healed so many but has created a firestorm of controversy
in the process.

I suspect that Nicodemus was looking for something to fill his
emptiness, as we all are. His was a religion of the head, not the
heart. As the name "Pharisee" implies, he was a "separated
one." He knew all of the dietary requirements and Sabbath
restrictions. He had renounced common pleasures in favor of
strict observance of the rabbinic law and traditions of the elders.
But something was missing. Chances are, Nicodemus was bored.
He had lost interest in the rituals; he had tired of the laws. Having emphasized outward performance for so long, he had
sacrificed his inward joy. He probably felt trapped. Not wanting
to tarnish his image as a religious leader, he struggled to keep
up appearances in the eyes of others but suffered from barren-
ness in his inner self.

In some ways Nicodemus reminds me of Brother Louie. A creation of radio's Garrison Keillor, Brother Louie is another man
whose faith was characterized more by outward rituals than by
inward power. In the fictional town of Lake Wobegon, Brother
Louie's car boasted Bible verses "across the dashboard, both
sunvisors, the back of the front seat, all four armrests, the rub-
ber floormats, the ashtray and glove compartment, and just in
case you weren't paying attention, he had painted a verse across
the bottom of the passenger side of the windshield—'The earth
is full of the goodness of the Lord'—for your edification as you
gazed at the scenery." Brother Louie's car was even equipped
with a horn that played the first eight notes of the Doxology
when he blew it.[1]

Why did Garrison Keillor include Brother Louie in his stories
from Lake Wobegon? I think it was because he wanted to show
how ridiculous an outward display of religion is without an inward relationship with God. Nicodemus seemed to sense that,
too.

Born for the Kingdom's Feast

Nicodemus comes to Jesus in search of an alternative to dead religion. Disillusioned with legalism, he yearns to move beyond the boredom syndrome. In response to his queries, Jesus tells him how his yearning can be satisfied: "Very truly, I tell you, no one can see the kingdom of God without being born from above" (John 3:3).

Jesus wants Nicodemus to see the difference between dead religion and living faith. To borrow an analogy from Jewish theologian Martin Buber, he wants him to see the difference between reading a menu and having dinner. Until you are born of God, you will always be an observer rather than a participant in the spiritual quest.

Yet the "menu" offered by religion may look so intriguing that the feast of transforming faith can be missed. Menus describe. They communicate information about the meals served by a particular restaurant. This is what religion does. It describes what God is like, what doctrines should be believed, what rituals should be practiced. Nicodemus had religion. As a Pharisee, he had been reading a menu for years, so preoccupied with knowledge *about* God that he had missed the joy that knowledge *of* God can bring.

So Jesus invites Nicodemus to discovery. In an extended conversation, he shares with him what it means to be "born from above." The Greek word translated "above" is *anothen,* which describes a radical spiritual change. Being born of God or born anew, as this word suggests, signifies such a total inner transformation that a paradigm shift occurs. A person moves from death to life, from religious boredom to relational bonding with God. The kingdom of God is at the heart of Jesus' message. He wants to enlist Nicodemus in the spiritual movement whose goal is cosmic wholeness. To cast the matter in Jungian language, as John A. Sanford does in his book *The Kingdom Within,* Jesus is talking about the establishment of "a higher moral and psychological consciousness."[2]

The rebirth that he commends to Nicodemus is the beginning of an adventure into a person's inner world. But the ego, the center of conscious life, resists this adventure. Corrupted by what Jung calls "the shadow" and Christians call "fallen human nature," the ego is vulnerable to the unhealthy attachments that cause addiction and alienate a person from God.

This is why conversion is necessary. Anyone who wants to maximize the power of the kingdom within must relinquish the selfish interests of the ego and embrace the higher purposes of the whole self, which is the potential for transcendence in each of us. Simply put, the conscious must be integrated with the unconscious. In order for this integration to occur, spiritual discipline is required. Periods such as Lent are essential. The fulfillment of personality that results from such discipline is so renewing that it can only be called being "born again."[3]

We long for this spiritual fulfillment. Whatever else we want from life, we want God more. Some time ago *Newsweek* magazine ran a cover story that made this point. Entitled "Talking to God," the story noted that, "Astonishingly, the current edition of *Books in Print* lists nearly 2,000 titles on prayer, meditation and techniques for spiritual growth—more than three times the number devoted to sexual intimacy and how to achieve it."[4]

More than a happy marriage, more than successful children, more than a satisfying career, even more than sexual intimacy, we want to know and be known by the One who loves us with an everlasting love. Receiving this love, being born anew, is more important to our well-being than friendship or knowledge, beauty or riches. To acknowledge this is the beginning of wholeness.

Jesus' conversation with Nicodemus assures us that what we want and need most, we can have. God meets us right where we are, amid all of our weaknesses and doubts and fears, to embrace us in intimacy. Lent reminds us that we respond by surrendering. It reminds us that the way of faith requires a radical bonding of the human spirit with God's Spirit. Lent initiates a journey of growth through which the heart is welcomed into the kingdom within.

A Celebration of Newness

Conversion takes place on two levels. The first is the level of spiritual rebirth that confirms one as a Christian; and second is the level of recurring catharsis that brings God near and promotes further surrender.

In the first sense, to be converted is to turn around and go in a new direction. This involves a change of lords. The person who has been under the lordship of self and sin comes under the lordship of God through faith in Christ. The resulting change of life is not merely intellectual; it is a radical transformation of personhood. As Paul says, "Everything old has passed away; see, everything has become new!" (2 Corinthians 5:17).[5]

The invitation to new life in Christ must be accepted personally. I can't do it for you; you can't do it for me. Pastor Maxie Dunnam relates the experience of William Gibson, author of *Mass for the Dead*. After Gibson's mother died, he longed for the faith that had sustained her throughout her life and upheld her in her courageous dying. Seizing his mother's dog-eared prayer book and putting on her gold-rimmed glasses, he sat in her chair and began to read. He prayed the prayers she had prayed because he wanted to hear what she had heard. He wore the glasses she had worn because he wanted to see what she had seen. He sat where she had sat because he wanted to feel what she had felt, to experience similar peace and empowerment. But nothing happened. Second-hand religion failed miserably. It always does.[6]

Compare Gibson's experience with John Wesley's journal entry for May 24, 1738, after he had attended a religious meeting on Aldersgate Street: "About a quarter before nine, while he was describing the change which God works in the heart through faith in Christ, I felt my heart strangely warmed. I felt I did trust in Christ, Christ alone for salvation; and an assurance was given me, that he had taken away *my* sins, even *mine;* and saved *me* from the law of sin and death."[7]

The words of Blaise Pascal, the scientific genius and Christian mystic, echo Wesley's experience. On a piece of paper, found in the lining of his coat after his death, Pascal had written an account of his conversion: "From about half past ten in the evening until about half past twelve, fire." Apparently Pascal carried the words with him as a reminder of how dramatically his new life in Christ began.

Drama is not required, however. Some Christians speak of their faith more as an evolution than a conversion. They recall gradually growing into a deep, heartfelt experience of Christ as Lord; they knew "no angel visitant, no opening skies," only the quiet assurance of having asked for mercy and received it. It is not as important how conversion happens but that it *does* happen. This joyful possibility is the hope celebrated during Lent, the season of the heart's rebirth.

The Wonder of Everyday Awakenings

Any conversion that is only a one-time experience is incomplete. To have a transforming effect, conversion must be ongoing. Conversion is a process through which fearful, doubting hearts encounter God in new and life-giving ways. Through such encounters, the heart is prodded to let go of one more subtle idol or one more besetting sin, negative attitude, or encumbering burden, to know the freedom of self-emptied commitment.

Martin Luther King, Jr., knew this freedom. During the historic bus boycott in Montgomery, Alabama, which launched the civil rights movement of the 1960s, he had a cathartic spiritual experience. As the leader of the boycott, he received many death threats from irate white racists. Late one night, he answered the phone to hear an ugly voice shout, "Listen, nigger, we've taken all we want from you! Before next week you'll be sorry you ever came to Montgomery!" The call unnerved him. Exhausted from the pressures of leadership, beset with fear, he wanted to quit. "I am at the end of my powers. I have nothing left. I've come to the point where I can't face it alone," he cried to God, head in hands, from the loneliness of his kitchen on that night of destiny.

What if God had not heard? There might have been no March on Washington, no freedom rides, no historic civil rights reforms. But God did hear. And King experienced the divine presence as never before. In his words, "I could hear the quiet assurance of an inner voice saying: 'Stand up for righteousness, stand up for truth; and God will be at your side forever.' Almost at once my fears began to go. My uncertainty disappeared. I was ready to face anything."[9] And face anything he did, all the way until his tragic death in Memphis in 1968. In responding to God's presence, he surrendered. Totally surrendered. The experience was like a new conversion; it moved his heart from fear to trust, from crisis to peace.

Such transcendent moments produce growth. They need not involve traumatic circumstances, but they always involve a life-altering response to God's presence. Bible study and prayer, weekend retreats, spiritual direction, psychotherapy—these are ways some people make this response. Others are born anew by responding to God in nature or art, by working for justice, or by finding intimacy with another person.

Signposts That Measure Progress

Cathartic spiritual experiences happen in countless ways, often to unsuspecting people in unlikely places. But dead religion cannot evoke them; only living faith can. Lent calls Christians to seize the opportunity to yield to rebirth. Such yielding will advance a person on the journey of growth that James Fowler describes in his book *Stages of Faith* and Kenneth Stokes elaborates in *Faith Is a Verb*.

The goal of this journey is what Fowler calls "universalizing faith." It is being in such harmony with God that values, beliefs, and actions become one. People at this stage feel bonded with all of humanity; they do not experience themselves as separate. Having experienced God not as external authority but as internal presence and power, they live beyond fear and addiction, deeply integrated, at one with their spiritual essence, centered in the peace of the kingdom within. Their sense of conscience leads them to challenge unjust social systems. Their commitment is total. Dietrich Bonhoeffer, Francis of Assisi, and Mother Teresa are models of universalizing faith.

To attain this level of growth, one must avoid getting stuck at a prior stage. Some people never develop a personal faith; they accept family or group beliefs without questioning them. This secondhand spirituality is characteristic of what Stokes calls the "innocent stage" of faith development. Those who do not believe that the Bible must be interpreted are at the "literalist stage"; those whose primary interest is in belonging to a group of like-minded people, at the "loyalist stage." Someone at the "critic stage" is struggling with the doubts and questions common during adolescence, a struggle necessary for growth but dangerous if it fosters disillusionment.

If one successfully progresses through Stokes's innocent, literalist, loyalist, and critic stages, one may become a "seer," integrating the best of the four previous stages into a faith that is intensely personal and truly "owned." Seers experience a deep sense of internal rightness or, to use the language of the Quakers, "clearness." Out of their harmonious inner core, they seek to treat others as they themselves would like to be treated. Not threatened by people different from themselves, they identify with the downtrodden and give of themselves in service.[10]

A very small percentage of seers eventually reach the level of universalizing faith (Stokes calls them "saints"). Jesus, more than anyone who has ever lived, reached this level. Having experienced the freedom of self-emptied commitment himself, he challenged others to surrender to God as he had.

This was his challenge to Nicodemus. It is also his challenge to us during this Lenten season. If we "seize the day," we can experience rebirth. In this experience lies the promise that these forty days can take us from the death of religiosity to enlivened spiritual relationship.

Prayer for the Second Sunday in Lent

To whom can I go but you,
        loving God,
            when I need someone who understands
            me better than I understand myself?

In your presence I feel welcome and wanted and whole.

You never treat me like a stranger who doesn't belong,
        but like an honored guest whose name is
        written in the Lamb's book of life.

When I am lost, you show me the way; when I am weak,
        you give me strength.

You often catch me unaware.

My faith is not deep enough or mature enough to keep me
        looking for your unexpected gifts of grace;
        I often miss them,
        or take them for granted.

And yet, even when I forget you,
        even when I put everything else first

and you last,
    you continue to love me.

Thank you for accepting me in Christ, just as I am.

I worship you as the God who invites me into
    the adventure of faith,
    who holds before me the possibility
    of new birth.

You call me beyond the ordinary and want more for me than
    the dreary monotony of the daily grind.

I hear your call when Jesus says, "Follow me."

But I often lack the courage to respond, the courage
    to take a stand for unpopular causes,
        to befriend marginal people,
            to give up besetting addictions.

In the silence of these moments,
    I seek an encounter with your Spirit.

I come wanting and needing to begin again,
    to choose, as if for the first time,
    your way, instead of the way of the world.

Help me to leave behind my destructive habits and attitudes.

Lead me on, during these days of Lent,
    to nurture what is best and highest in myself
    by surrendering to what is best and highest
    in you. Amen.

Questions for Reflection and Study

1. Do you identify with Nicodemus's experience of ritualistic
    faith? What factors might contribute to the formation of
    faith that is nominal or impersonal rather than alive and
    growing? How big a factor is boredom? In what ways may
    it be more dangerous to a person's spiritual health to be a
    nominal Christian than an unbeliever?

2. Martin Buber used the analogy of reading a menu versus eating dinner to describe the difference between religion and spirituality. Can you think of other analogies that might be used? In your own words, describe the difference between living faith and dead religion.

3. John 3 is one of the few chapters in the Bible that contains the phrase "born from above." Is this an essential concept in your understanding of what it means to be a Christian? Explain why or why not. Can someone whose spiritual development evolves slowly over time still be "born from above"?

4. Look at other places in the Bible that make reference to conversion. (See, for instance, Ephesians 1:3-14, where Paul uses terms such as "redemption," "adoption," and being "in Christ"; Romans 6:1-11, where he describes the Christian life as dying and rising with Christ; and 2 Corinthians 5:16-21, where he speaks of "everything old" passing away. See also the references to "darkness and light" in 1 John 1:5-10 and 2:7-11; and passing "from death to life" in 1 John 3:14). How do these passages complement or contradict the idea of being "born from above"? Why is it important to emphasize conversion during Lent?

5. Are there hints in Jesus' conversation with Nicodemus that he was talking about the establishment of "a higher moral and psychological consciousness," as John Sanford suggests?

6. Have you ever had a "cathartic spiritual experience" such as the one that Martin Luther King, Jr., had? If so, share it with the group and tell what you learned from it and whether or not it continues to inform your faith experience.

7. Dietrich Bonhoeffer, Francis of Assisi, and Mother Teresa are mentioned in this chapter as models of what James Fowler calls "universalizing faith." Can you think of others? How might Lent move one in the direction of universalizing faith?

8. Reflect on the stages of faith mentioned in this chapter. Where do you see examples of these in the church today? How might a knowledge of these stages help you in assessing your own spiritual development or in working with other Christians?

Notes

[1]Garrison Keillor, *Lake Wobegon Days* (New York: Viking Penguin, 1985), 115.

[2]John A. Sanford, *The Kingdom Within* (San Francisco: Harper San Francisco, 1987), 37.

[3]Ibid., 12.

[4]"Talking to God," *Newsweek* (January 6, 1992), 40.

[5]See the article on "Conversion" by F. Laubach, J. Goetzmann, and U. Becker in *The New International Dictionary of the New Testament*, ed. Colin Brown, 3 vols. (Grand Rapids: Zondervan, 1975-78), 1:355.

[6]Maxie Dunnam, *That's What the Man Said* (Nashville: Upper Room, 1989), 24.

[7]Quoted in F.F. Bruce, *The Epistle of Paul to the Romans* (Grand Rapids: Eerdmans, 1977), 59.

[8]Quoted in Bruce Larson, *The Presence: The God Who Delivers and Guides* (San Francisco: Harper and Row, 1988), 21.

[9]Martin Luther King, Jr., *Stride Toward Freedom* (New York: Harper and Row, 1958), 133-135.

[10]For a description of the stages of faith development, see James W. Fowler, Stages of Faith: *The Psychology of Human Development and the Quest for Meaning* (New York: Harper and Row, 1981); Kenneth Stokes, *Faith Is a Verb: Dynamics of Adult Faith Development* (Mystic, Conn.: Twenty-Third Publications, 1989); and Charlotte Davis Kasl, *Many Roads, One Journey: Moving Beyond the 12 Steps* (New York: Harper Collins, 1992).

3

Unexpected Grace for Unsuspecting People

A Reading from the Gospel According to John (4:5-26)
So he came to a Samaritan city called Sychar, near the plot of
ground that Jacob had given to his son Joseph. Jacob's well was
there, and Jesus, tired out by his journey, was sitting by the well.
It was about noon.

A Samaritan woman came to draw water, and Jesus said to her,
"Give me a drink." (His disciples had gone to the city to buy food.)
The Samaritan woman said to him, "How is it that you, a Jew, ask
a drink of me, a woman of Samaria?" (Jews do not share things
in common with Samaritans.) Jesus answered her, "If you knew
the gift of God, and who it is that is saying to you, 'Give me a
drink,' you would have asked him, and he would have given you
living water."

The woman said to him, "Sir, you have no bucket, and the well
is deep. Where do you get that living water? Are you greater than
our ancestor Jacob, who gave us the well, and with his sons and
his flock drank from it?" Jesus said to her, "Everyone who drinks
of this water will be thirsty again, but those who drink of the water
that I will give them will never be thirsty. The water that I will give
will become in them a spring of water gushing up to eternal life."
The woman said to him, "Sir, give me this water, so that I may
never be thirsty or have to keep coming here to draw water"

Jesus said to her, "Go, call your husband, and come back." The
woman answered him, "I have no husband." Jesus said to her, "You
are right in saying, 'I have no husband'; for you have had five

husbands, and the one you have now is not your husband. What you have said is true!" The woman said to him, "Sir, I see that you are a prophet. Our ancestors worshiped on this mountain, but you say that the place where people must worship is in Jerusalem." Jesus said to her, "Woman, believe me, the hour is coming when you will worship the Father neither on this mountain nor in Jerusalem. You worship what you do not know; we worship what we know, for salvation is from the Jews. But the hour is coming, and is now here, when the true worshipers will worship the Father in spirit and truth, for the Father seeks such as these to worship him. God is spirit, and those who worship him must worship in spirit and truth." The woman said to him, "I know that Messiah is coming" (who is called Christ). "When he comes, he will proclaim all things to us." Jesus said to her, "I am he, the one who is speaking to you."

Show me a person who dislikes adventure, and I will show you someone intimidated by life and frustrating to be with. We all know such people. They are the ones who won't go anywhere without a thermometer, a hot-water bottle, and an umbrella.

Lent comes to challenge this timidity, to restore life's daring. It does this by celebrating the unexpected, especially in relationships. As Christians journey from Ash Wednesday to Easter Sunday, they share Jesus' trials and triumphs. A bond forms with him and with each other amid the unfolding drama of redeeming grace.

An old Jewish legend captures the mystery of this developing bond. Many years ago in Palestine there were two brothers who owned a farm together. They shared everything equally— the work as well as the profits. Each had his own barn. One of the brothers was married with children; the other brother was single. One day while working in the field, the single brother was struck with pangs of guilt. He thought to himself, "It is not fair that we divide the grain evenly. My brother has a family to support; I have only myself." He decided to remedy the inequity by taking a bag of grain from his barn each night and secretly putting it in his brother's barn.

Meanwhile, the married brother was also feeling guilty. It occurred to him that in his old age his children would take care of him, while his brother would be all alone. He also decided to take a sack of grain from his barn each night and secretly place it in his brother's barn.

Morning after morning both brothers were amazed that, although they had removed a sack of grain from their barns, none was ever missing. Then an incident occurred to explain the mystery. One night when they were halfway between their barns, each carrying a sack of grain, their paths crossed. According to the legend, the brothers embraced and gave thanks for each other. At that moment, God looked down from heaven and said, "I declare this to be a holy place." It is said that this was the spot on which Solomon built the first temple.

The two brothers received grace from each other. Their feelings of mutual concern became concrete in action. Such unmerited favor produces security in relationships, and secure people are no longer afraid to take the risks necessary for adventurous living. Rather than fearing the unexpected, they welcome it.

This is why Christians need a season of Lent. Lent provides opportunities for spontaneous spiritual encounters. Such encounters teach that, although human relationships often falter and cause pain, our relationship with God remains as stable as our faith is persistent. As Easter's dawn breaks, illuminating the meaning of Christ's cross, it announces the triumph of grace and invites believers to live in the amazing freedom it inspires.

A scene beside an old well in the country of Samaria communicates one of Lent's powerful lessons. Jesus, passing by on his way from Judea to Galilee, has a conversation with a Samaritan woman. Their conversation emphasizes the need for risk in group relationships and honesty in personal ones. When we develop these qualities, we begin bonding internally with ourselves, relationally with others, and spiritually with God; boredom is banished, and the adventure of faith renewed.

High on the Wings of Risk

Picture the scene where the conversation takes place. A forbidding Samaritan landscape swelters in the heat of the Middle Eastern sun. The hour is noon. Jesus is hungry, thirsty, and tired from his travels. His disciples have gone into town to buy food, and he waits alone. Seeking refuge beside an old well, he encounters a woman of Samaria.

Longstanding bitterness existed between Judeans and Samaritans, who were neighbors as well as kinsfolk. The bitterness began in centuries of warfare during the period of the divided kingdom after Solomon's death. The destruction of the main Samaritan religious shrine on Mount Gerizim by the army of John Hyrcanus in 128 B.C. raised hostilities to a fever pitch. To the Samaritans, the Torah alone was Scripture. They revered Moses even more than the Jews did. But they rejected the temple at Jerusalem, believing that the Scriptures declared Mount Gerizim as its rightful place. For holding these unorthodox beliefs, and for intermarrying with foreigners, the Jews condemned the Samaritans. The Samaritans, on the other hand, hated the Jews because of their cruelty in the past and their refusal to treat them as equals.

Jesus also faced another problem as he met the woman at the well: The sex roles of the day prohibited him from speaking to her in public. "Do not converse much with women as this will ultimately lead you to unchastity," warned the rabbis in the Talmud. Intensifying the warning, Jose ben Johanan of Jerusalem, who lived around 160 B.C., wrote, "He that talks much with womankind brings evil upon himself and neglects the study of the Law and at the last will inherit Gehenna."[2]

In New Testament times women were defined by their sexuality rather than their intelligence or character. Their primary role was to bear children and maintain the home. They were seen as inferior, the weaker sex. As such they were thought to be incapable of spiritual understanding and lacking inherent value. Apart from a man, a woman had no means of support or identity.

Jesus transcends all these prejudices, however. Putting oppressive conventions aside, he not only asks the Samaritan woman for a drink and spends significant time with her but also engages her in a deep discussion about spiritual matters. He takes a risk in order to build a bridge of understanding where none previously existed.

A Conspiracy of Goodness

Jesus' actions proclaim the kingdom of God, which promises

justice and equality for all people. Ending bigotry based on race, class, age, or sex, the kingdom inaugurates a new order of harmony. In this order the disinherited find hope and power in community. Each person is treated as a unique individual. Respect for human dignity flourishes. Everyone has enough food for the body, enough enlightenment for the mind, and enough liberation for the spirit to grow toward wholeness.

Unfortunately, the kingdom often seems distant from today's world. When 1 percent of a country's richest people control nearly one third of its wealth, as in the United States today, this creates social hostilities inconsistent with kingdom values. When the United States leads the world in per-capita incarceration of criminals at a rate of 426 people per 100,000 residents, its citizens are not heeding the kingdom's call to reconciliation. When over one hundred thousand women are raped each year and the homeless population numbers somewhere between half a million to five million persons, such injustices undermine the kingdom's vision of security and compassion.[3]

Still, the kingdom's promise cannot be thwarted; one day the promise will be fulfilled. When Jesus risked his reputation as a man, a rabbi, and a Jew to speak with the Samaritan woman, he declared his belief in this ultimate fulfillment. Behind his words stood the conviction that, although the kingdom may seem distant, it is by no means dead—and is nearer than we think. The order of strife and violence may reign for a moment, but God's peace will triumph in eternity.

I confess that sometimes I find it hard to believe in this triumph. In a world of dissension and division, peace is elusive. Even amid the worst conflicts, however, a witness to peace can be found if one looks for it through the eyes of faith. Consider the 1992 Los Angeles riots. The injustice of the Rodney King verdict sparked an equally unjust response of the massive burning, looting, and killing. God's peace seemed as absent as chastity in a brothel. By the time order was restored, $1 billion worth of property damage had been done to Korean, African American, Caucasian, and Hispanic businesses; five thousand jobs had been lost; and an estimated fifty-three people had died.

A dramatic television news clip of a gang of blacks beating a white truck driver named Reginald Denny came to epitomize the brutality of the riots. It seemed that racial hatred had claimed another victim as Denny was shot, punched, pummeled with a fire extinguisher, and left for dead.

But that's not how the story ended. Four brave people—all African American—came to his aid. Lei Yuille was the first to arrive at the corner of Florence and Normandy, where the beating occurred. She climbed into the cab of the truck with Denny and became his "eyes" as he attempted to drive to safety while nearly blinded and only half-conscious. Later, Bobby Green, a truck driver who had seen the beating on television, intercepted the vehicle and took over at the wheel. He was led to the hospital by Titus Murphy and Terri Barnett, who cleared a path through the riot-torn streets with their car. Dr. Madison Richardson, a black neurosurgeon, and an interracial medical team that included Dr. Richardson's white associate and a Korean anesthesiologist, were able to save Denny's life.

These people built bridges of peace across a stormy racial divide. Their actions embody the hope of God's kingdom. Whenever good triumphs over evil or right perseveres against wrong, whenever humanity's oneness is affirmed and its divisions healed, the kingdom is present.

An extraordinary book entitled *Rescuers: Portraits of Moral Courage in the Holocaust* by Gay Block chronicles another arena in which courageous people built bridges of peace. The book contains interviews with over one hundred of the unsung heroes who risked their lives to save Jews from the Nazi death camps by hiding them in their homes or apartments or on their farms. In reflecting on their rescuing activities, one Dutch couple said, "We didn't think about it. . . . You started off storing a suitcase for a friend, and before you knew it, you were in over your head." Christine Gorman of *Time* magazine described these acts of heroism as "a conspiracy of goodness." As a result, as many as half a million lives were saved—all because some ordinary people were willing to take the risk.[4]

Jesus participated in the conspiracy of goodness when he spoke to the woman at the well. Reaching out to her across the cultural, sexual, and religious barriers that separated them, he dramatized the hope of liberation. Lent reminds Christians that a cross may await those who follow his example. These forty days invite us to hear—and heed—the gospel's call to daring action, in spite of the consequences.

Lent also has a message for this age of diminishing resources.
The message warns that neighbor will always live in fear of
neighbor until more people build bridges that unite instead of
barriers that divide. Rich against poor, white against black, Arab
against Jew, straight against gay, male against female, conser-
vative against liberal—these animosities will be healed only
through a revolution of love. Without this revolution, competition for necessities such as jobs and housing, education and
health care will continue to create hostilities between groups.
In this climate, bigotry and violence thrive.

Lent is a time for reflecting on the kingdom's promise of a better day. It is a time for joining Jesus in risking all for others, even
if what lies ahead is a cross.

Getting Honest About Getting Hurt

The healing of society and the healing of the individual go hand
in hand. One cannot be accomplished without the other. Listen
further to Jesus' conversation with the Samaritan woman, and
you will hear this point confirmed.

The conversation gets personal—even invasive! Jesus probes
the woman's marital history, which she tries to keep secret.
Despite her attempted denials, he confronts her with the truth.
She has been married not once, not even two or three times; this
woman has had five marriages and now lives with a man who
is not her husband. She has learned from her own experience
how difficult intimate relationships can be.

The closer you are to me, the more you see my flaws and shortcomings. The closer I am to you, the more I notice your weaknesses and idiosyncrasies. It takes a concerted and often painful effort to make an intimate relationship work; that's the
nature of commitment. Five times the Samaritan woman and the
men to whom she was married failed. And five times they paid
the price of interpersonal alienation and emotional upheaval.

When it comes to trauma, psychologists say divorce and the
death of a loved one are equally devastating. But Christine
Archambault, cofounder of Divorce Anonymous, points out a
major difference: "After your divorce, no one brings a cas-
serole . . . . everybody takes a couple steps backward. Or they'll

say things like, 'I knew at the wedding it wouldn't last.' "

Had the Samaritan woman endured this humiliation? Had her heart been broken repeatedly, leaving her scarred and hurting? I find it hard to believe otherwise. As is true of any major loss, divorce leads to bereavement, a word meaning "to be dispossessed." Someone in bereavement has lost something precious that can never be replaced. Such losses initiate periods of grief that are depressing at best; at worst, they plunge the spirit into despair.

German theologian Dorothee Söelle experienced this despair when her marriage ended. "It took me three years to overcome and come to terms with the suicidal thoughts and desires that filled my mind," she wrote in her book *Death by Bread Alone.* "I was crying out for help, and the only kind of help I could conceive of or want was that my husband would come back to me, or that I would die and my misery would be over and done with."[6]

For Bonnie Kreps, an award-winning filmmaker and journalist, the despair hit when her partner abruptly announced, "The spark is gone." There was, Kreps recalls, "no warning, no explanation then or later; I was, simply, *out.* In shock, I fled. . . . The pain was excruciating. During the first week of my sanctuary I had nightmares every night and woke devastated by what I had dreamt."[7]

The Samaritan woman had probably known similar pain. Though John gives no details about her five marriages or how they ended, we know that in the Greco-Roman world men initiated most divorces and had the most to gain from them. In some cases divorce left women jobless and homeless. What a predicament! No work and no shelter in a world hostile toward women. Is this what happened to the Samaritan woman? Had she become bored with one husband after another, or they with her? Did she and her husband always reach the point of having nothing to talk about over dinner? Had they gotten stuck on the treadmill of spending time with the same old friends, stewing over the same dissatisfactions? Worse, had this pattern of disintegration repeated itself in relationship after relationship, leaving her so embittered against marriage that she spurned it in favor of a live-in lover? Despite the cultural differences between our two worlds, I find it easy to imagine this scenario.

Face the Truth, Find Your Future

The Samaritan woman's story was shaped by unhealthy shame. How could it not have been? She had failed to meet society's expectations. An outstanding wife and mother—that's what she was supposed to be, but wasn't. Instead, her record marked her as the queen of dysfunctional relationships. Was it her fault? It didn't matter. All that mattered was the humiliation she felt, the humiliation that made her life as barren as the Samaritan hills.

Helen Block Lewis, a respected psychiatrist, suggests that shame and depression are closely linked. People ashamed of who they are attack their own personhood. Why? Because they internalize the feelings of worthlessness that they think others project on them. Whether they realize it or not, their disgust for themselves verifies the old maxim, "I am not what I think I am. I am not what you think I am. I am what *I think you think* I am." Filled with the self-loathing that becomes inner torment, shame-based people denigrate themselves in the presence of others. Not only do they engage in chronic negative thinking, they also fall prey to addiction and other self-destructive behaviors.[8]

In the *Bloom County* cartoon strip, the little penguin named Opus experiences shame when some members of the community find him reading certain magazines. He is charged with penguin lust and expelled from the Bloom County kingdom. The exiled Opus hangs his head and shuffles off to the far corners of the world. Sometime later, he finds employment as a male penguin stripper, the only job of which he feels worthy. "I am suffering," he says, "from chronically and fatally low self-esteem."[9]

My guess is that feelings of worthlessness plagued the Samaritan woman. This is evident in her subtle evasiveness with Jesus. She has something to hide, a dark secret that she has been carrying for years and never able to accept or share. Jesus nudges her toward honesty by speaking the truth about her marital indiscretions. Her response—"Sir, I see that you are a prophet"—indicates spiritual growth and a deepening awareness of who he is.

"To tell your secrets, to experience thus the human commu-

nion which we all need" is the ultimate goal of all psychotherapy, according to Swiss psychiatrist Paul Tournier.[10] By
listening to the woman and accepting her just as she is, Jesus
helps heal her brokenness and give her a new future. In the end,
she becomes a changed person. Leaving her water jar and going
back to the city, she says to the people, "Come and see a man
who told me everything I have ever done!"

She still has the same problems she had before, to be sure, but
now she has a new spirit and faith with which to solve them. By
taking her from boredom to bonding with him, Jesus helps her
believe in herself again. Her self-worth restored, she discovers
what an adventure life can be when guided and empowered by
faith in Christ the Messiah.

Lent is a time for coming to Jesus Christ in search of a similar
transformation. The search involves a renewed effort to
eliminate the barriers of race and sex and class that divide the
human community. It involves deepening one's spiritual
discipline through increased commitment to the social values of
God's kingdom.

Lent is also a time for personal growth, the growth that begins
with uncompromising honesty. As we transcend denial and admit our failures, we find that God's grace in Christ is sufficient
to sustain us in all circumstances. Befriended by the One who
befriended the woman of Samaria, Easter's dawn begins to
break in our hearts. In the light of this dawning, each new day
holds more promise than the one before.

Prayer for the Third Sunday in Lent

O Thou who art from everlasting to everlasting,
    the same yesterday,
      today,
        and forever,
    I center myself in you.

You are the God of the morning light and evening shade,
    of spreading galaxies afar off
    and purple mountain majesties close at hand.

In your presence I see life not only as it is,
        but as it could be.

You remind me that I was created not to be bored,
        but to be reborn.

Why do I often settle for less?

Why do I allow unworthy goals,
            unhealthy people,
                unruly passions,
        to have power over me?

I come to you, O Lover of My Soul,
        to realign my spirit with your Spirit.

You know my thoughts before I think them;
        you understand my feelings before I express them;
        you share my burdens before I carry them.

In you I find that my dark and barren winters of
        despair can become bright and
        glorious springtimes of hope.

I thank you for meeting me right where I am,
        in all my dignity and all my shame,
            all my promise and all my inadequacy,
            all my turmoil and all my peace.

Even though I sometimes feel empty, Lord,
        like a well that has gone dry,
        you promise me living water.

Keep me walking the Lenten road of faith
        that I might drink this water
        in the brilliance of Easter's dawn.

Especially when the way is hard,
        and the temptation to turn back strong,
        lift up my eyes to the hills
        and remind me where my help comes from.

Fix my eyes on Jesus,
        the pioneer and perfecter of my faith,
        "who for the sake of the joy that

was set before him endured the cross,
    disregarding its shame,''
and has taken his seat
    at your right hand.

May I remember that he loved me so much in death
    that he offered me a crown of life,
    and may that life deepen and grow in me
    today and every day. Amen.

Questions for Reflection and Study

1. This chapter began with a story about two brothers and the
    amazing grace they received from each other. What is your
    response to this story? How might it be understood as a
    parable of the Christian life? Have you ever experienced
    anything similar? If so, what did your experience teach you
    about the wonder of God's grace?

2. To understand the meaning of Jesus' conversation with the
    Samaritan woman, it is important to emphasize the animosi-
    ty that existed between the Jews and the Samaritans. Can
    you think of animosities between groups in today's world
    that are similar? How might the biblical conversation have
    sounded if it had occurred between an Iranian and an Iraqi?
    a Catholic and a Protestant in Northern Ireland? a black and
    a white in South Africa? a Serb and a Muslim in the former
    Yugoslavia?

3. Biblical scholars agree that the kingdom of God was at the
    heart of the message of Jesus. In what ways did Jesus bear
    witness to the kingdom in his conversation with the woman
    at the well? How is Jesus' witness relevant to today's discus-
    sions about gender roles, race relations, and other situations
    in which how we treat one another is an issue?

4. What does this chapter suggest about the relationship be-
    tween healing society and healing an individual? Do you
    agree that one cannot be accomplished without the other?

What can the church do to help people see these two emphases as a unity? How might Lent be a time of such opportunity?

5. Although we cannot say for sure that boredom was a factor in the breakup of the Samaritan woman's marriages, what role do you think boredom plays in the stagnation of marriages and other relationships today? Are our expectations that relationships be exciting and fulfilling realistic? What are some ways that boredom's effects might be neutralized? How might Lent become a season for infusing new life into dying relationships?

6. Experts have suggested that shame is an underlying cause of addiction. Do you agree or disagree that shame was a problem for the woman of Samaria? How might the gospel of God's grace in Christ offer possibilities for healing?

7. Was Jesus' conversation with the Samaritan woman consistent in tone with conversations he had with other people in the Gospels? How was her self-esteem affected by his refusal to condemn her? Did Jesus ever condemn anyone or call anyone a sinner? If not, what does his approach suggest for how the gospel should be preached today?

Notes

[1] Cited in Mary J. Evans, *Woman in the Bible* (Downers Grove, Ill.: InterVarsity Press), 35.

[2] Cited in Aida Basancon Spencer, *Beyond the Curse* (Nashville: Thomas Nelson, 1985), 55.

[3] See "America's Bulging Prisons," *Christian Science Monitor* (January 24, 1991), 20; Lee Michael Katz, "Rapes Reach 'Epidemic' Rate in 1990," *USA Today* (March 22-24, 1991), 1; and Kurt Shillinger, "U.S. Program to House Homeless Lags," *Christian Science Monitor* (November 15, 1991), 3.

[4] Christine Gorman, "A Conspiracy of Goodness," *Time* (March 16, 1992), 65-67.

[5] Quoted by Terry Lee Goodrich, "Divorce by the book," *Providence Journal-Bulletin* (October 23, 1991), E-1, E-4.

[6]Dorothee Söelle, *Death by Bread Alone*, trans. David L. Scheidt (Philadelphia: Fortress Press, 1978), 32.

[7]Bonnie Kreps, *Subversive Thoughts, Authentic Passions* (San Francisco: Harper and Row, 1990), 6.

[8]Ronald Potter-Efron and Patricia Potter-Efron, *Letting Go of Shame* (San Francisco: Harper and Row, 1989), 66.

[9]Melody Beattie, *Beyond Codependency and Getting Better All the Time* (San Francisco: Harper and Row, 1989), 105.

[10]Paul Tournier, *Secrets* (Richmond, Va.: John Knox Press, 1965), 40.

4

To See with the Eyes of Your Soul

A Reading from the Gospel According to John (9:1-25)
As he walked along, he saw a man blind from birth. His disciples asked him, "Rabbi, who sinned, this man or his parents, that he was born blind?" Jesus answered, "Neither this man nor his parents sinned; he was born blind so that God's works might be revealed in him. We must work the works of him who sent me while it is day; night is coming when no one can work. As long as I am in the world, I am the light of the world." When he had said this, he spat on the ground and made mud with the saliva and spread the mud on the man's eyes, saying to him, "Go, wash in the pool of Siloam" (which means Sent). Then he went and washed and came back able to see. The neighbors and those who had seen him before as a beggar began to ask, "Is this not the man who used to sit and beg?" Some were saying, "It is he." Others were saying, "No, but it is someone like him." He kept saying, "I am the man." But they kept asking him, "Then how were your eyes opened?" He answered, "The man called Jesus made mud, spread it on my eyes, and said to me, 'Go to Siloam and wash.' Then I went and washed and received my sight." They said to him, "Where is he?" He said, "I do not know."

They brought to the Pharisees the man who had formerly been blind. Now it was a sabbath day when Jesus made the mud and opened his eyes. Then the Pharisees also began to ask him how he had received his sight. He said to them, "He put mud on my eyes. Then I washed, and now I see." Some of the Pharisees said,

"This man is not from God, for he does not observe the sabbath."
But others said, "How can a man who is a sinner perform such
signs?" And they were divided. So they said again to the blind
man, "What do you say about him? It was your eyes he opened."
He said, "He is a prophet."

The Jews did not believe that he had been blind and had received his sight until they called the parents of the man who had
received his sight and asked them, "Is this your son, who you say
was born blind? How then does he now see?" His parents
answered, "We know that this is our son, and that he was born
blind; but we do not know how it is that now he sees, nor do we
know who opened his eyes. Ask him; he is of age. He will speak
for himself." His parents said this because they were afraid of the
Jews; for the Jews had already agreed that anyone who confessed
Jesus to be the Messiah would be put out of the synagogue.
Therefore his parents said, "He is of age; ask him."

So for the second time they called the man who had been blind,
and they said to him, "Give glory to God! We know that this man
is a sinner." He answered, "I do not know whether he is a sinner.
One thing I do know, that though I was blind, now I see."

The parents at Weihsien camp had a problem. It all started
with their assignment to the "Civilian Internment Center" in
Shantung Province, China, during that country's war with
Japan. The time was the early 1940s. As U.S. and British citizens
working in China, they had been taken captive by the Japanese.
This they expected. What they didn't expect was what happened to their families as a result of their confinement. While
the parents stole precious moments of privacy in their one-room
living quarters, their teenagers went out and became involved
in illicit sexual activity.

Telling the story in his book *Shantung Compound*, Langdon
Gilkey explains that the problem arose because "camp life is,
on the surface, intensely dreary and boring. There is nothing
new, unusual, or really fun to do; the day is filled with un-
pleasant chores. Consequently, teenagers found themselves continually bored, looking around for something, *anything*, exciting."

How could the parents solve such a thorny problem? Left to
themselves they had no workable answer. Enter Eric Liddell,

whose story was told in the award-winning film *Chariots of Fire*. After winning the 440 in the Olympics for England in the 1920s, he had come to China as a missionary. Now in his forties, he had been interned at Weihsien camp and become known for his overflowing enthusiasm, good humor, and love of life.

Rather than seeing the teenagers' rebelliousness as a problem, Liddell saw it as an opportunity. He initiated a program of activities that drew them to the game room in their spare time. He helped them build model boats, directed them in square dancing, challenged them to games of chess, and otherwise poured himself out to capture the minds and imaginations of the penned-up youths.

Gilkey says of Eric Liddell (whom he calls "Eric Ridley" to protect his identity), "It is rare indeed when a person has the good fortune to meet a saint, but he came as close to it as anyone I have ever known."[1] When Liddell was stricken with a brain tumor and died shortly before the encampment ended, everyone, especially the youth, mourned for days, so great was the vacuum created by his death.

When Sight Is Better Than Sainthood

Eric Liddell was one of those rare souls who reached James Fowler's stage of universalizing faith. His faith enabled him to see life in an internment camp not only as it was but as it could be. Theologian Stanley Hauerwas says this is also Christianity's goal: to teach us to see as God sees.

Lent should help Christians advance toward this goal. If used to break boredom's power by infusing new life into dead routines, Lent can heal the soul's blindness. Since clarity of vision is the key to wholeness in the spiritual life, this healing is of critical importance. Only those who really see can know where they are going. They alone can avoid stumbling over the obstacle of temptation or wandering into the blind alley of disillusionment. As Indian writer Margaret Chatterjee was fond of saying, "If you don't know where you are going, any road will get you there."

Observing Lent as a spiritual perfectionist doesn't help one learn to see as God sees. I have tried it; it got me nowhere. My attempts to give up bad habits, worldly pleasures, and rich foods left me feeling like the man who went to his doctor complaining of a headache. The doctor promised to give him something to stop the pain after asking the man a few questions. "Tell me," said the doctor, "do you drink much liquor?"

"Liquor?" snapped the man indignantly. "I never touch the filthy stuff."

"Do you smoke?"

"I think smoking is disgusting. I've never had a cigarette in all my life."

"How about staying out late at night or eating sweets and fattening foods?"

"Nope. I watch my diet carefully, and I'm in bed every night by ten o'clock at the latest."

"Tell me," probed the doctor, "does this headache you complain of involve a sharp, shooting kind of pain?"

"That's right," said the man, "a sharp, shooting kind of pain."

"Simple, my dear man! Your problem is that you have your halo on too tight. All you need to do is loosen it a bit and your headache will go away."

Something is amiss if Lent promotes the "halo effect," inspiring legalism and spiritual pride. What is more, if I am filled with guilt when I indulge in that which I vowed to give up, I have allowed my Lenten observance to go awry.

I do not want to feel either proud *or* guilty; I want to feel healthy and whole during Lent, as in all seasons. In order to accomplish this, I need vision. When I see Jesus more clearly, I bond with him and become whole in his love and grace. That's not to say that giving up certain foods or substances or attitudes is wrong—not at all! But fasting only deepens one's faith when combined with positive steps to follow Christ more closely. Lent takes us beyond the ordinary when it produces in us a vision of his life and energizes us to imitate it.

A Message in Mud and Mercy

Christ's healing of the man born blind in John 9 emphasizes how essential vision is for the adventure from boredom to bonding. Blindness deprives a person of color and light, of the freedom to walk without stumbling, of the ability to match a friendly voice with a familiar face.

The life of the blind in first-century Palestine was mired in morose monotony. Each day repeated the ordeal of the day before—the ordeal of struggle and humiliation. In order to eat, the blind had to beg. Dressed in rags, smelling of the streets, with disheveled hair and forlorn faces, they congregated in city squares and along the highways and byways to ask for money from the passersby. "Have mercy!" was their cry; "Help me, please!" their lament. As if the grinding poverty of their miserable condition were not degrading enough, their suffering prompted questions from the religious people of the day. Who sinned, the pious wanted to know, that these people should have been born blind?

The disciples asked this question of Jesus when they encountered a blind man in Jerusalem during the Feast of Tabernacles. (What better time for Jesus to give a sign of who he was!) No one sinned, he answered them. This man was born blind "so that God's works might be revealed in him" (John 9:3). And indeed they were!

Jesus proceeded to make mud from the ground and spread it on the man's eyes. I can visualize the Master's hands: those of both carpenter and Great Physician—calloused yet nimble, steady yet creative, gentle yet confident. As strong as they are sensitive, these hands reach out and touch; they invite and welcome. They are hands that encourage and comfort, restore and heal. The hands of Jesus, so eternal yet so personal—they communicate the love and power of God. The blind man goes to wash in the pool of Siloam, as instructed, and comes back seeing! No one can disprove or explain the miracle. It all happened to show God's works through Jesus, the light of the world, who came "for judgment so that those who do not see may see, and those who do see may become blind" (John 9:39).

It is noteworthy that the Bible records only Jesus giving sight to the blind. He performs this kind of healing more than he makes the lame walk, the deaf hear, the dumb speak, or does any other miracle. No one in the Hebrew Scriptures had the power to restore sight; only God is said to have it. Nor do the disciples heal blindness in the New Testament.[2] The implication of all of this is that Jesus and God are one.

Toward a Kinder, Gentler Faith

Lent becomes a transforming season when we seek Christ's healing for the spiritual blindness that manifests itself in the form of intolerant religion. These forty days dramatize the problem because intolerance was one of the factors that caused Jesus' crucifixion by making it politically expedient.

The story of the man born blind shows the intolerance of the Pharisees. This is sad because at their best much about them was admirable. The Pharisees were devout followers of the law who courageously preserved Judaism after the temple was desecrated by the Greeks under Antiochus Epiphanes. They also tirelessly defended their faith against the pagan beliefs and morals of the Romans. In these instances they acted heroically.

But they were also extremists. The Pharisees loved their traditions and wanted to pass them on, but they feared dissent. This made them hostile toward Jesus, whose radical faith called their motives into question and threatened their identity. Fear led the Pharisees to persecute the man who had been healed from blindness. Convinced that the healing was a hoax, they did their best to discredit his story and spurn Jesus. Twice they interrogated the man, demanding a detailed explanation of what happened. They even called in the man's parents in the hope of proving his story false. The attempt failed when they could not refute his simple testimony about Jesus: "I do not know whether he is a sinner. One thing I do know, that though I was blind, now I see" (John 9:25). In frustration, they finally became enraged and drove the man out.

Such reactionary responses occur when people's emotions short-circuit their reasoning abilities. When blinded by fear and prejudice, they cannot see the truth. People emotionally attached to toxic religious ideas will not forsake them, no matter how destructive the ideas are shown to be. Some engage in unethical and extreme actions in religion's name. This happens when addictive dependencies and unbridled passions sabotage clear thinking. The problem exists in all organized religions; Christianity is no exception.

As a student in South Africa, Mahatma Gandhi became deeply interested in the Bible, especially the Sermon on the Mount. Soon he was convinced that Christianity held the answer to the suffering caused by India's caste system, and he considered becoming a Christian. In his autobiography he tells of going to church one Sunday to learn more. When he got there, he was stopped at the entrance and told that if he wanted to attend worship, he was welcome to do so in a church reserved for blacks. He left and never returned.

Many years later, Howard Thurman, the distinguished African American Baptist minister, visited Gandhi at his ashram in India. Before they parted, Thurman asked him what he believed to be the greatest obstacle preventing the spread of Christianity in India. Gandhi answered, "This is the greatest enemy that Jesus Christ has in my country—not Hinduism, or Buddhism, or any of the indigenous religions—but Christianity itself."[3]

An important step is taken on the Lenten journey when the gospel's ideals are affirmed but the abuses committed in Christ's name renounced. Theologian Reinhold Niebuhr explained these abuses—crusades, sectarianism, bigotry, and the like—as outward expressions of an inward idolatry. This idolatry, at the heart of all human evil, happens when the worship of one's own self or group replaces the worship of the true God revealed in Jesus Christ.

In this age of uncertainty, beset by intense competition between nations and peoples, humanity's inner idolatry is often expressed in acts of violence. Economic hard times lead some to look for scapegoats. Groups such as the skinheads and neo-Nazis have burgeoned in this volatile climate, attracting a following among alienated youths who blame their problems on religious, ethnic, or sexual minorities. The legacy of these groups has been an increase in hate crimes on a worldwide scale.

Those who perpetrate these crimes fail to see that they are hurting themselves in the process. As novelist Robert Penn Warren says through his character Jack Burden in *All the King's Men*, ". . . the world is like an enormous spider web and if you touch it, however lightly, at any point, the vibration ripples to the remotest perimeter." Intolerance and violence have a ripple effect that touches everyone, not only the perpetrators and victims but the entire human family. In a hostile environment, neither social nor personal wholeness can flourish. As long as one person lives in fear and oppression, we will all be fearful and oppressed.

Unfortunately, every heart harbors its share of bias. Why do we find it hard to accept those who are different from us? Because we are insecure ourselves. If we know who we are, as Jesus did, we are not threatened by another person's culture or race, beliefs or lifestyle. We are able to live our lives and let them live theirs, at peace with one another. Such peace begins with inner approval. When I accept myself as radically and unconditionally as God accepts me in Christ, I am empowered to accept you as well. I stop competing with you and start loving you. I stop fearing you and start honoring your personhood. Having taken these positive steps, I am no longer alienated from you but ready to be your friend.

Lent enhances our ability to bond with others by deepening our bond with Christ. The more secure we are in him, the more understanding we become of those different from ourselves— and the less likely we are to run aground on the shoals of boredom. One cannot be bored when celebrating the marvelous diversity of humanity. Instead one catches a new vision of God's kingdom and joins Jesus on the adventure toward it, prepared to endure the cross in order to share in resurrection life.

Less Than Christ Is Never Enough

Another result of the blindness of the Pharisees was their tendency to mistake life's good gifts for its best gifts. The temple and its traditions were good but not the best. The allegiance of the Pharisees to the law blinded them to the surpassing worth of Christ's grace.

Not that observing the law was bad. By no means. This observance elevated Jewish morality to majestic heights. The commandments to protect the weak and preserve human dignity were a source of stability and hope. These commandments unified the Jewish community; they gave the people meaning and direction.

But the law was not supposed to be an end in itself, only a means to the end of knowing God and making God known. In turning the law into an idol, the Pharisees obeyed its letter but violated its spirit. Thus they were unprepared to recognize God's greatest gift, Jesus Christ.

Their mistake is easy to make, especially in the United States of America, the land of abundance, where good gifts often pass for the best. I think of this when I remember the reaction of Vasily Miroshnichenko when he first came to the United States. Miroshnichenko is an immigrant from Latvia. Shortly before the breakup of the Soviet Union, he arrived here with his wife, his eighty-year-old mother-in-law, and four of his six children and began attending the church I serve as pastor. For the first several weeks he was here, he was constantly in tears. He wept for joy when he came to church without government harassment. He wept when he saw the overstocked shelves at the supermarket. He wept when he got an American job and drove an American car and held his American-born granddaughter for the first time. Having had so little, he was overwhelmed by the experience of having so much.

America, the land of so much! We live in the nicest homes, drive the fastest cars, shop in the biggest malls, attend the finest schools. But although we have the highest standard of living in the world, "so much" is not the best. Danger lurks. It's the danger of becoming so preoccupied with what we own, and so comfortable with our lifestyle, that we forget God and neglect the poor.

One can find oneself subscribing unconsciously to the philosophy of the bumper sticker that says, "Whoever has the most stuff wins." That philosophy blinds people to the truth that happiness is not found in possessions; it's found in the liberating relationships with others and God and self made possible by the cross of Christ. This is the higher happiness for which we were created and for which our famished spirits hunger.

A story is told of an Amish man who momentarily stopped working in his field to watch a new neighbor move in. Among the neighbor's household items were a deluxe refrigerator with a built-in ice-cube maker, a high-tech stereo system with a compact disk player, a remote-control television with VCR, and a whirlpool hot tub.

The next day, the Amish man and his wife paid their new neighbor a visit. They took him homemade muffins and jam, extended a warm welcome, and engaged him in friendly conversation. When it was time to go, the Amish man offered, "If anything should go wrong with any of your appliances or equipment, don't hesitate to call me."

"That's very generous of you," said the new neighbor. "Thank you!"

"No problem," the Amish man replied, "I'll just tell you how to live without them."

One need not be Amish to doubt that possessions can bring happiness; one need only see with the eyes of the soul. Without this inner vision, the good will be mistaken for the best, and life will be grounded by boredom rather than soar on the wings of adventure.

Boredom is inevitable whenever life's material and spiritual spheres do not intersect. Christians believe that the intersection happened, and happens anew, in Christ. That's what Lent affirms. Lent comes to transform our perspective, to give us new eyes with which to see body and soul as a unity. Without this spiritual vision, we are likely to turn money, sex, and power into idols and to create oppressive social systems as a result. It is the suffering caused by these systems that makes God seem absent and injustice eternal.

This is why we need a season of Lent: to help us remember that all things are being made new in Christ. Through the lens of his cross, Christians see life not only as it is but as it could be—and will be—when love's redeeming work is complete. Lent gives us a vision of eternity's wholeness beyond time's brokenness, of Easter's triumph beyond Calvary's tragedy.

Lent affirms that God is not absent but is continually seeking us—just as Jesus, upon hearing of the healed blind man's inter-rogation by the Pharisees, sought him. Finding the man, Jesus asked him, "Do you believe in the Son of Man?" (John 9:35). After some initial confusion, the man answers, "Lord, I believe." Then he worships him. Lent's purpose is to bring us all to this point of recognition and worship. Having arrived there, our spiritual blindness will be healed, and along with it, our boredom, for we will have bonded with Christ and begun an adventure beyond the ordinary.

Prayer for the Fourth Sunday in Lent

O God of miracles and mysteries,

I rejoice that nothing in all of creation
can separate me from your love.

Even when the eyes of my soul are blind because
I have lacked the faith to open them,
I am held in your embrace.

You never let me go.

You never turn me away.

Although I cannot see you,
I hear your voice in my inner spirit.

In spite of the sound and fury of the world
that rings constantly in my ears,
in spite of the clamor of many competing distractions,
your voice breaks through.

It is a gentle voice,
soft yet persistent,
understanding yet challenging,
that comforts me when I am disturbed,
and disturbs me when I am comfortable.

Penetrate my defenses and speak to me anew, O God.

Come as the wind that refreshes,
the rain that cleanses,
the fire that refines.

I lay bare before you the best and worst of myself.

Part of me yearns to know you,
to do your will.

Another part of me resists you.

It wants to be left alone—
alone to enjoy the pleasures of its addictions,
to savor the rewards of its compromises,
to bask in the smugness of its pride.

I bring both parts of me into your presence, gracious God.

Heal the blindness of my soul,
that, in seeing you as you are,

I might see myself as I am,
and affirming the good and vowing
to change the bad, become whole.

Let me never forget
that in the gospel of our Lord Jesus Christ,
the night is far spent and the day is at hand.

When storm clouds gather and shadows fall,
teach me not to be afraid.

Remind me that
beyond the darkness of life's many crosses,
lies the radiance of Easter's dawn.

Open my eyes to see this dawn even now,
and give me faith to believe in the
new heaven and new earth that you promise
your people, in whom the risen Lord lives.
Amen.

Questions for Reflection and Study

1. This chapter presents Christianity as a discipline in learning how to see, as theologian Stanley Hauerwas suggests. Eric Liddell saw an internment camp and the teenagers in it not as they were, but as they could be. Was this also Jesus' approach? Give examples of his efforts to bring out the best in people, and discuss how these efforts were related to his vision of God. If you believe that God is trying to bring out the best in *you*, how will this affect your life and faith?

2. Do you feel that Lent is most valuable as a time for denying oneself or as a time for improving one's spiritual vision? Are the two mutually exclusive? What are some ways to accomplish the latter?

3. Christianity becomes boring to those whose spiritual insight is not continually getting sharper, much like boredom may be a problem for some who are physically blind. Do you agree or disagree?

4. What significance do you give to the fact that only God and Jesus restore sight to the blind in the Bible? What about the fact that Jesus performed this miracle more than any other?

5. The disciples asked Jesus, "Rabbi, who sinned, this man or his parents, that he was born blind?" (John 9:2). Is this a legitimate question? What kinds of misunderstandings might result from the theology behind it?

6. Observe the response of the Pharisees to the man who had received his sight. Why were they unable to believe his story? Why did they treat him so badly? Can you think of situations in which Christians behave in a similar manner?

7. Reinhold Niebuhr attributed various forms of hatred and intolerance to the human tendency toward inward idolatry. What did he mean by this? How might this inward idolatry be redirected into positive expressions of spirituality?

8. Do you agree or disagree that boredom is basically a spiritual problem? What are some ways in which we settle for life's good material gifts and miss God's best gift of a growing relationship with Christ?

Notes

[1]Langdon Gilkey, *Shantung Compound* (New York: Harper and Row, 1966), 190-92.

[2]See Leon Morris, *The Gospel According to John* (Grand Rapids: Eerdmans, 1971), 475.

[3]Howard Thurman, *With Head and Heart* (New York: Harcourt, Brace, Jovanovich, 1979), 135.

[4]Quoted in Robert Drake, "Robert Penn Warren's Enormous Spider Web," *Christian Century* (November 22, 1989), 1089.

[5]Story from Bernie Siegel, as cited in *Pulpit Resource*, vol. 19, no. 4 (October/November/December 1991), 20-21.

5

A Bash for an Adventure Gone Bust

A Reading from the Gospel According to Luke (15:1-3,11-32)
Now all the tax collectors and sinners were coming near to listen to him. And the Pharisees and the scribes were grumbling and saying, "This fellow welcomes sinners and eats with them." So he told them this parable: . . . "There was a man who had two sons. The younger of them said to his father, 'Father, give me the share of the property that will belong to me.' So he divided his property between them. A few days later the younger son gathered all he had and traveled to a distant country, and there he squandered his property in dissolute living. When he had spent everything, a severe famine took place throughout that country, and he began to be in need. So he went and hired himself out to one of the citizens of that country, who sent him to his fields to feed the pigs. He would gladly have filled himself with the pods that the pigs were eating; and no one gave him anything. But when he came to himself he said, 'How many of my father's hired hands have bread enough and to spare, but here I am dying of hunger! I will get up and go to my father, and I will say to him, "Father, I have sinned against heaven and before you; I am no longer worthy to be called your son; treat me like one of your hired hands."'

So he set off and went to his father. But while he was still far off, his father saw him and was filled with compassion; he ran and put his arms around him and kissed him. Then the son said to him, 'Father, I have sinned against heaven and before you; I am no longer worthy to be called your son.' But the father said to his slaves, 'Quickly, bring out a robe—the best one—and put it on him; put a ring on his finger and sandals on his feet. And get the fatted calf and kill it, and let us eat and celebrate; for this son of mine was dead and is alive again; he was lost and is found!' And they began to celebrate.

Now his elder son was in the field; and when he came and approached the house, he heard music and dancing. He called one of the slaves and asked what was going on. He replied, 'Your brother has come, and your father has killed the fatted calf, because he has got him back safe and sound.' Then he became angry and refused to go in. His father came out and began to plead with him. But he answered his father, 'Listen! For all these years I have been working like a slave for you, and I have never disobeyed your command; yet you have never given me even a young goat so that I might celebrate with my friends. But when this son of yours came back, who has devoured your property with prostitutes, you killed the fatted calf for him!' Then the father said to him, 'Son, you are always with me, and all that is mine is yours. But we had to celebrate and rejoice, because this brother of yours was dead and has come to life; he was lost and has been found.' "

Except for the news and sports, I find little on commercial television worth watching. Very few programs inform and enlighten as well as entertain, and the shows that are the most popular often appeal to the dark side of human nature. But I am an addict. I use television as a narcotic to help me escape stress, loneliness, or monotony. I sometimes find myself watching a program that I have no real interest in, just to have something to do. In a phrase, my secret motto is, "When the going gets tough, the tough turn on the tube!"

When I put this motto into practice, I am inevitably confronted with images that make my life seem boring. "L.A. Law" reminds me how boring a career in the ministry is compared with the high drama of the courtroom. "Wheel of Fortune" reminds me that I have a boring income. The guests on "Phil Donahue" suggest that I have boring values, and the characters on "Cheers" and "Murphy Brown" imply that I have a boring love life.

The commercials are even worse! Their unspoken message is that I drive a boring car, wear boring clothes, eat boring food, drink boring beverages, and will forever remain a hopelessly boring person unless I buy the advertiser's product and use it religiously.

On most days I am unaffected by all of this sleazy propaganda, but once in a while, in weaker moments, I succumb to its appeal. An inner voice seems to whisper, "Maybe the TV propagandists are right. Maybe your life *is* boring." When I listen to this voice and believe its accusation, I become susceptible to temptation.

In an effort to escape my boredom, to introduce a little adventure into my life, I begin to desire the scintillating images, glittering lifestyles, and extravagant products I see on television. Captivated by this desire, if not in action then in spirit, I leave my inner place of meditation and wander into the "distant country" of attachment, a sojourner adrift from my home in God.

The Promise Beyond the Pigpen

Because of my tendency to stray, I sympathize with the predicament of the prodigal son in Jesus' classic parable. He seemed to have it all—comfort and security, youth and ambition. But one thing he lacked: adventure! A painful conversation with his father was all that stood between him and the intoxicating freedom of the open road. I imagine the conversation starting calmly enough but generating sparks of animosity in short order. I can hear the father calling his younger son "irresponsible" and the son bristling and escalating the argument into a high-stakes war of words.

"If I'm irresponsible, then you're unreasonable!" shouts the son. "You expect too much of me. I'm tired of following your orders and obeying your rules and hearing your criticisms. I'm bored to tears with life at home. I want my freedom! Give me my inheritance and let me seek my fortune on my own."

There is a long pause. Finally, with deep sadness in his eyes, the father turns to his son and says, "All right. We have argued enough. Two people can only take so much pain. Have it your way. If you are determined to leave, I will not try to stop you."

And leave he does. Traveling hard and fast, the son takes his inheritance and hits the high road to what he thinks will be the adventure of his life. No one to answer to, no curfews, no chores! Instead, he finds pain and crisis in the distant country, where he loses everything—his money and ambition, his confidence and self-respect. Alone and in despair, he takes a job feeding pigs—an unspeakable humiliation for a Jewish boy—and finds himself hungry enough to envy their food. At the end of his rope, he decides he has no alternative but to go home and hope his father will take him in.

Meanwhile, his father has continued working in the fields each day, often stealing glimpses into the distance, in hopes that he will see his son returning home. But each day, all that he can see is a deserted landscape and the dust hanging heavy in the stagnant air.

Months pass before the scene finally changes. Then suddenly, as if from out of nowhere, the son appears. The father can hardly believe his eyes. He drops everything, lets out a shout of joy, and runs to greet the returning prodigal. They weep, they embrace, they stand back to look at each other and embrace again, this time holding on as if to never let go, as if to communicate in silence feelings too deep for words. Then comes the father's order to his servants, " 'Quickly, bring out a robe—the best one—and put it on him; put a ring on his finger and sandals on his feet. And get the fatted calf and kill it, and let us eat and celebrate; for this son of mine was dead and is alive again; he was lost and is found!' " (Luke 15:22-24).

What a meaningful story for Lent, the season for getting honest with ourselves and God! These forty days challenge us to acknowledge how often we go astray. They declare that we are all prodigal sons and daughters, prone to wander into sin and despair, yet welcomed and embraced by God when we finally come back home.

Why Driven People Run Out of Gas

Lent's call to discipline and renewal reminds us of our vulnerability to the allure of the "distant country," each of us in our own way. Personally, I feel most vulnerable when I'm dissatisfied with my life. When victimized by boredom's subtle yet powerful effects, I abandon my spiritual center in search of excitement amid tedium, fullness amid dullness.

The pursuit of anything less than God will leave me broken in the distant country; I know that. Yet the influence of my fallen nature is so strong that I habitually engage in these pursuits. Success and pleasure, power and money, knowledge and approval—these become my idols. Instead of following Christ on the inward adventure toward surrender, I seek fulfillment in externals, in the evasions and illusions and seductions of addicted living. Thus I become a driven person; my life spins out of control, and I head for a fall.

Tragically, I don't even realize it. In this state of lost awareness, I become like the man who called a taxi to pick him up immediately. When the cab arrived, he rushed out of his house, jumped into the back seat, and shouted, "Drive!"

"Where to, sir?" asked the driver.

"Anywhere," came the reply, "and hurry!"

Following the impulses of the lower nature rather than living as a new creation in Christ leads nowhere fast. But Lent's gift is what author Arthur Gordon calls "the power of purposeful pausing"—a fresh opportunity, through prayer and self-examination, to hear God's voice and give up one's idols once and for all.[1]

Beware of Everyday Watergates

Unless Lent's opportunity is seized, the Christian journey gets easily sidetracked. This is especially true in today's world of sophisticated temptations. Human nature has not changed, but the moral context at the close of the twentieth century has.

The hero of Frank Moorhouse's wry novel *Forty-Seventeen* describes this context when he exclaims, "Let us drink to the discipline of indiscipline which must guide us all in every action."[2] I can almost hear the wine glasses ringing in celebration of this paradoxical toast in many quarters of American life. The tragedy is that "indiscipline" leads people and nations into the distant country of moral and spiritual ruin. The seeds of ruin germinate in the home when husbands and wives lose control of their emotions or fail to teach their children responsibility. Indiscipline makes schools ineffective, businesses unproductive, governments chaotic. Without discipline, tempers flare in tense neighborhoods, and sex and violence reign in the media.

In short, indiscipline takes a devastating toll on character. People allow themselves to be controlled by their baser instincts rather than their spiritual essence. They fail to set proper boundaries or heed danger signs that they are going astray. Radio minister Charles Swindoll uses the analogy of the warning light on the dashboard of a car. When the engine overheats, the light glows red. The prudent person will stop the car and look under the hood to see what is wrong; the fool will smash the light with a hammer and keep on driving.

In the United States, we have been using the hammer method for so long that we no longer recognize the symptoms of spiritual wanderlust, let alone the underlying problem of making idols of externals instead of worshiping God. Thus, like the prodigal son, we are helpless to resist the attraction of the distant country.

Columnist Jonathan Rowe gave a specific example of the effects of indiscipline in an editorial that appeared some time ago in the *Christian Science Monitor.* Rowe suggested that the Keating Five scandal was worse than Watergate. How could this be? Because the senators known as the Keating Five, who accepted campaign contributions from Charles Keating in exchange for political favors on behalf of his beleaguered Lincoln Savings and Loan, were only doing business the way it is done daily in high places. Watergate involved a sensational crime committed once; the Keating Five scandal involved the corruption of the everyday. Because of its subtler and more pervasive effects, commonplace dishonesty is more dangerous than spectacular deceit because no one notices it until it has already wreaked its devastation.

In the Keating Five case, the indiscretions of a few senators worsened the savings-and-loan debacle, which will cost every U.S. family five thousand dollars a year for ten years. The debacle could have been prevented if those involved would have known their limits and lived within them, but they did not have the discipline to do it. Without discipline, evil gets out of hand and destroys people before they even realize what is happening.[3]

This is how many of us become God's prodigal sons and daughters. Few of us commit the heinous crimes reported on the evening news; we are not hardened criminals. But amid the ordinary, "the world is too much with us," as Wordsworth said. We are plagued by everyday corruptions of the spirit. Superficial relationships, constant haste, besetting addictions, unloving words and actions—these are but a few of the habits that alienate us from God.

The Book of Common Prayer, stalwart of Anglican worship since the Reformation, contains this honest admission: "We have erred and strayed from thy ways like lost sheep. We have followed too much the devices and desires of our own hearts. . . . We have left undone those things which we ought to have done; and we have done those things which we ought not to have done." Indiscipline in everyday living makes such a confession necessary. The confession acknowledges our tendency to become drifters in the distant country of wasted potential.

Although the sins of the everyday immobilize the strongest of Christians, Lent promises that these sins can be overcome by a renewal of faith. Experiencing God's presence afresh empowers one to conquer indiscipline. It is an empowerment rooted not in the negative fear of punishment but in the positive pursuit of wholeness and joy.

When You Have to Look Up to See Bottom

In order to reach this positive place, one may have to endure great pain, as the prodigal son did. His rebelliousness and lavish living brought him face to face with despair—a living hell! Imagine being reduced to feeding the pigs, to being a totally broken person. That's the predicament in which he found himself.

Most of us need not imagine such brokenness; we have experienced it in our own way. For instance, rejection in relationships causes intense pain. Sartre, the French existentialist, described this experience in his play *No Exit*. Three people, all victims of unrequited love, are trapped in a room with no way of escape. The man loves the first woman, but she loves the second woman, who loves the man. Hell is spending eternity in this condition of unfulfilled desire.[4]

Or what about failure? At times even the most confident and gifted person goes down in defeat. As a Yiddish proverb says, "From misfortune to fortune is a long way. From fortune to

misfortune is but a step.'' When you have failed in your career
or marriage, when you have let yourself and others down as a
leader or friend or parent, you find yourself in the minihell of
self-blame and regret.

The many ways we run from God lead us into the distant country. Like the prodigal son, we take our spiritual inheritance and
squander it. For some, the squandering is done through drugs,
crime, or casual sex; for others, through bad choices or misplaced
priorities, negative attitudes or spiteful actions. Whenever we
live unconsciously, failing to seek first God's kingdom, we risk
losing all.

Others, however, end up in despair through no fault of their
own. I have become aware of this in working with people who
were abused as children or grow up in dysfunctional families.
Someone else's addiction or unhappiness, rage or emotional in-
stability wounded them. It was not their fault. And yet, they
must live with deep scars and many questions, the most haunting of which is, "Why me?" Profoundly hurt, they wander in
the distant country of brokenness, feeling estranged from God
and the warmth of human caring. The loneliness of their struggle can be heard in the words of Daddo, a character in Leon
Uris's novel *Trinity*, when he says:

> We live . . . with a number of rooms inside us. The best room
> is open to the family and friends and we show our finest face in
> it. Another room is more private, the bedroom, and very few are
> allowed in. There is another room where we allow no one in . . .
> not even our wives and children, for it is a room of the most in-
> timate thoughts we keep unshared. There is one more room, so
> hidden away that we don't even enter it ourselves. Within we lock
> all the mysteries we cannot solve and all the pains and sorrows
> we wish to forget.[1]

Because Daddo's words express the silent anguish of inner
alienation, they speak to us all. We invite this anguish when we
fight or flee intimacy with God and join the prodigal son in the
distant country. God's unconditional love should comfort and
heal us, and often does. But we also fear this love. We are afraid
it will stifle our fun and freedom, that it will make too many
demands on us or confine us in ways we cannot predict.

So we rebel. We run. We hide. Too proud to answer to anyone
else, we take self-reliance so far that we abandon our spiritual

roots and begin living in the desolate land of moral compromise and emotional distress. Jesus' parable is so powerful because what the younger son brought on himself is what we bring on ourselves when we prefer any other experience to intimacy with God.

This Way to the Time of Your Life

Thankfully, the climax of the story is not at the beginning, where the boy demands his inheritance and leaves home. The climax is not in the distant country either, where desperation sets in. The story's high point is at the end, in the joyful reunion of father and son. Like a loving parent, God aches to embrace those who abandon their spiritual roots but then admit their folly and return home again. No matter how far we have wandered, God forgives and forgets in Jesus Christ and receives us with thanksgiving.

I have been helped by what the late Leslie Weatherhead, a pastor of the famous City Temple in London during World War II, suggested to his congregation. He advised that they remember the acronym "LUFA" as a reminder of the phrase "I am *L*oved, *U*nderstood, *F*orgiven, and *A*ccepted in Jesus Christ." When I follow Weatherhead's recommendation and think of this phrase in the morning, as the water of the shower runs over my body, I feel cleansed not only outwardly but inwardly. I begin the day affirmed by God, confident that no problem will defeat me.[2]

That we are loved, understood, forgiven, and accepted in Christ is Lent's promise, communicated in the message of the cross and the empty tomb. Christ died and rose again to bring us all—all who like sheep have gone astray—back home. A growing relationship with him will not solve all of our problems or make our lives perfect. But it will heal our aloneness. It will take us on an adventure beyond the ordinary and transform our boredom with life into bonding with God.

When this happens, we feel more secure and at peace than ever before. Problems become opportunities; relationships, channels of grace. Through the enlightened eyes of faith, the future looks bright and the present challenging. Knowing *who* we are because we know *whose* we are, we bring light into the world's darkness. A bond of oneness develops between us and our sisters and brothers in the human family because we feel deeply bonded to our own spiritual selves. The empowerment and energy unleashed within us as a result of this bonding makes boredom unlikely and growth inevitable. For the first time in our lives, we are whole and free.

The legendary French painter Matisse had already lived three-quarters of a century when he wrote of his art, "It's as if I have all of life before me, after all, all of another life."[3] Similarly, to come home to God's love in Christ is to reinvent the present and the future. A process of rebirth is initiated; the shame of the past is forgotten. What better season than Lent to rejoice in the welcome that awaits us as God's prodigal sons and daughters!

Prayer for the Fifth Sunday in Lent

Most high and holy God,
>you have brought me to this time and place
>on my journey of faith.

When I was wandering far from you,
>enslaved by my darker passions,
>you waited patiently for me to come back home.

Confidence in your long-suffering love gave me
>the courage to take my first
>tentative steps toward you.

You greeted me with open arms.

You welcomed me as your long-lost child,
>even as you welcome me now,
>>rejoicing in our reunion,
>>embracing me with tears,
>>ordering a celebration.

No matter how much is yet unresolved in my life,
>no matter how many loose ends still dangle,
>I am learning to rest in your presence.

I want to live just for today,
>to grow beyond who I was yesterday,
>to stop worrying about tomorrow.

O God of time and eternity,
>   because all things begin and end with you,
>   I can let go of my need always to be in control.

I can turn over my life to your care and keeping,
>   knowing that I am safe in the hollow
>   of your hand.

You have given me the gift of grace in Jesus Christ.

In the blessed communion of prayer,
>   I receive the gift again with thanksgiving.

You have brought me this far by faith, O Lord;
>   take me farther still, I pray.

Help me grow beyond the unhealthy dependencies
>   and incriminating inconsistencies that
>   bind my spirit.

Remind me that growth occurs
>   not through increased effort
>   but through deeper surrender.

May I learn that any experience can serve a
>   good purpose if I trust you in the midst of it.

Therefore, let me not forget to thank you for
>   the fears and tears,
>   the foes and woes,
>   the problems and pains
>   that come my way, intermingled with
>   the joys and successes,
>   for each has its role to play in
>   teaching me to seek first your
>   kingdom. Amen.

Questions for Reflection and Study

1. Think about the relationship between the season of Lent and the parable of the prodigal son. In what ways can we grow spiritually during Lent by acknowledging our tendency to stray from God? How might we grow by deepening our

understanding of God's grace? Are there other themes in Jesus' parable that you hear more clearly or powerfully during this season than in others because you hear them against the backdrop of Jesus' passion?

2. Although not discussed in this chapter, the response of the elder brother to the return of the prodigal son is also rich in meaning. Do you identify with him? If not, explain why not. If so, address the question of why his predicament is relevant to a Christian during Lent. John Sanford in *The Kingdom Within* suggests that the two brothers can be understood not as separate individuals but as two sides of a single personality. Are these two sides present in you?

3. Do you find the tension between the father and his younger son believable? In your opinion, was Jesus describing what today would be called a "dysfunctional family"? Does this parable suggest anything about Jesus' realism concerning family relationships? Did the father do the right thing in giving his son his inheritance? What effect would it have on the story to change the parent figure to a mother?

4. The problem of indiscipline was a theme in this chapter. Do you agree or disagree that brokenness often results from a failure to maintain control of our fallen human nature? Do you respond positively or negatively to the idea of a disciplined life? How would your spiritual life be affected if you thought of discipline more as a means of attaining joy than of avoiding trouble?

5. Reflect on the utter humiliation that the prodigal son felt as a Jewish boy having to feed the pigs to survive, even envying them their food. Can you think of times in your life when you experienced similar brokenness because of your own bad choices? If so, what role did guilt play in your restoration? Discuss the difference between healthy and unhealthy guilt and how they affect your relationship with God.

6. Do you agree or disagree that sometimes we end up in the "distant country" of pain and brokenness because of what others have done to us rather than because of our own waywardness? Does the Bible suggest any ethical guidelines or inner personal disciplines that might help one recover from this condition?

7. Reflect on the statement about our inner rooms made by Daddo in *Trinity* by Leon Uris. Does his insight ring true to your experience? How might the biblical/psychological idea of "bonding with one's redeemed self" help you to transcend the sense of isolation that Daddo's statement describes?

Notes

[1]Arthur Gordon, *A Touch of Wonder* (Guideposts, 1974), 211-213.

[2]Frank Moorhouse, *Forty-Seventeen* (Orlando: Harcourt Brace Jovanovich, 1988), 8.

[3]Jonathan Rowe, "Worse Than Watergate," *Christian Science Monitor* (January 3, 1991), 11.

[4]I am indebted for this reference to Bruce Larson, *Living Beyond Our Fears* (San Francisco: Harper San Francisco, 1990), 63-64.

[5]Leon Uris, *Trinity* (New York: Bantam Books, 1976), 59.

[6]See Leslie D. Weatherhead, *Key Next Door* (New York: Abingdon, 1959), 29.

[7]Quoted in Louise Sweeney, "Distillations of a Lifetime of Art," *Christian Science Monitor* (September 7, 1989), 10.

6

Christ's Cross My Challenge

A Reading from the Gospel According to Mark (15:1-25)
As soon as it was morning, the chief priests held a consultation with the elders and scribes and the whole council. They
bound Jesus, led him away, and handed him over to Pilate. Pilate
asked him, "Are you the King of the Jews?" He answered him,
"You say so." Then the chief priests accused him of many things.
Pilate asked him again, "Have you no answer? See how many
charges they bring against you." But Jesus made no further reply,
so that Pilate was amazed.

Now at the festival he used to release a prisoner for them,
anyone for whom they asked. Now a man called Barabbas was in
prison with the rebels who had committed murder during the in-
surrection. So the crowd came and began to ask Pilate to do for
them according to his custom. Then he answered them, "Do you
want me to release for you the King of the Jews?" For he realized
that it was out of jealousy that the chief priests had handed him
over. But the chief priests stirred up the crowd to have him release
Barabbas for them instead. Pilate spoke to them again, "Then
what do you wish me to do with the man you call the King of the
Jews?" They shouted back, "Crucify him!" Pilate asked them,
"Why, what evil has he done?" But they shouted all the more,
"Crucify him!" So Pilate, wishing to satisfy the crowd, released
Barabbas for them; and after flogging Jesus, he handed him over
to be crucified.

Then the soldiers led him into the courtyard of the palace (that is, the governor's headquarters); and they called together the whole cohort. And they clothed him in a purple cloak; and after twisting some thorns into a crown, they put it on him. And they began saluting him, "Hail, King of the Jews!" They struck his head with a reed, spat upon him, and knelt down in homage to him. After mocking him, they stripped him of the purple cloak and put his own clothes on him. Then they led him out to crucify him. They compelled a passer-by, who was coming in from the country, to carry his cross; it was Simon of Cyrene, the father of Alexander and Rufus. Then they brought Jesus to the place called Golgotha (which means the place of a skull). And they offered him wine mixed with myrrh; but he did not take it. And they crucified him, and divided his clothes among them, casting lots to decide what each should take.

It was nine o'clock in the morning when they crucified him.

Sometimes, when I hear about the latest North American craze—from off-track betting to sports-card trading, from self-help psychologizing to bungee jumping—I am tempted to agree with American satirist H. L. Mencken: "No one ever went broke underestimating the intelligence of the American people." But I am usually not that cynical. I am more inclined to believe that a paralyzing sense of boredom, not a lack of intelligence, explains the American gullibility for gimmicks.

Never has a people been more addicted to fads. The American love affair with the chic and trendy is legendary. We have a weakness for the latest fashions and prettiest faces, the slickest advertising and sappiest music, the glitziest celebrities and juiciest gossip. An endless array of diversions caters to our insatiable need to be entertained, to be delivered from boredom's curse. We seem to hope that keeping ourselves preoccupied in this way will help us forget our inner emptiness and alienation.

I was struck by how boredom can become toxic when I saw a front-page news item in the *Wall Street Journal* about the state where I live. I was amazed to read that "the Central landfill in Johnston, Rhode Island, attracts more than 200 people a week, ranging from cub scouts to foreign dignitaries . . . Since April, 7,000 people from 33 states and 20 foreign countries have toured the landfill and recycling plant."[1]

Granted, attempts to dispose of garbage in an environmentally responsible way are interesting. But two hundred people a week at a landfill? How ironic! To think that in this media-blitzed, gotta-have-a-gimmick land of twenty-four-hour-a-day entertainment, some people are still so bored that a visit to the dump seems exciting. This is revealing. Perhaps it says something about the entertainment diet Americans are being fed—that it's a junk food diet at best. In fact, even real junk, the kind found in landfills, is more likely to keep one from getting bored.

What People Who Have Everything Still Need

The human spirit cannot soar to great heights without more substantial nutrition. The gnawing loneliness inside each person is a longing for God, a hungering and thirsting that nothing else can satisfy. Boredom is a spiritual problem; it cannot be solved through material means.

All of the blazing conflagrations on movie screens, all of the nail-biting drama in suspense novels, all of the sensuous movement on rock videos, all of the passionate melodies on the hit parade, the sensational tabloid headlines, the double-overtime playoff heroics—these provide a thrill a minute to their devotees. But beyond the thrill, there is emptiness.

Lent's call is to something deeper and more lasting. It is a call to come to the water of life and drink until one's thirst for wholeness is quenched. It is a call to come to God's banqueting table of freedom, to eat until one's soul finds peace.

We began these forty days with Jesus in the desert. He transcended boredom and the temptations that came with it by bonding with God's will through God's word. Then we saw how boredom affected Nicodemus and the Samaritan woman, the blind man and the prodigal son—and how grace helped them live beyond it.

Now we come to the place of ultimate challenge and commitment: the cross of Christ. It is here that redemption's drama engages the mind and stirs the heart most profoundly. Anyone touched by the mystery of this drama will be changed. The mystery involves time and eternity, judgment and mercy, estrangement and intimacy. As hymnist Isaac Watts wrote, "See, from his head, his hands, his feet, sorrow and love flow mingled down! Did e'er such love and sorrow meet, or thorns compose so rich a crown?''

When one encounters "the wondrous cross," as Watts did, boredom ends because bonding begins. It is a bonding between the human heart and the very heart of God. Though it may seem peculiar that an instrument of torture could inspire such passionate affection, this is part of the mystery. The wonder of suffering love creates faith that expresses itself in reverence and praise.

Whenever I think of the cross amid the ordinary affairs of my life, I am moved. It may seem morbid to meditate on a scene of execution, but in this case the scene is so extraordinary that such meditation is not morbid but illuminating. When I think of the cross, I increase my awareness of how deep God's love for me goes. I remember that I am a sinner saved by grace. I celebrate the hope of forgiveness, the promise of new and abundant life.

To meditate on these things fills my spirit with gratitude and joy for what Jesus did for me. The message of the cross is always relevant. In it I find the support that sees me through the stress of the everyday. Thinking about the cross elevates my spirit to the level of worship; instead of being bored, I am uplifted and challenged.

Mark's Gospel records the essential facts about Christ's death as an historical event: "Then they brought Jesus to the place called Golgotha (which means the place of a skull) . . . And they crucified him" (Mark 15:22-24). Simple words, yet unfathomable in meaning. This was no ordinary death because Jesus was no ordinary person. According to the church's time-honored teaching, he was truly God, truly human, truly one.

Futility Is Trying to Fly with Broken Wings

But why did Jesus have to die? What does the cross really mean? The simple answer is that he died to save us from our sins. We cannot save ourselves. No matter what progress is made in fields from science to agriculture, from medicine to computer technology, human nature remains the same--fundamentally flawed. The twentieth century, a time of stellar achievement, has also been the bloodiest in all of history.

Sin is not only breaking God's law of love, although it is certainly that; it is also failing to reach one's full potential. Thinking in terms of "dos and don'ts" trivializes sin, distorting its deeper meaning as the condition of brokenness in which all of humanity lives. As theologian Gabriel Fackre explains, "Sin is the code word in the Christian story for the turning inward of the self, and thus the turning away from God, neighbor, and nature. . . , an 'ego trip' inward, rather than a pilgrimage outward and ahead toward the horizon of Shalom."[2]

The shalom about which Fackre speaks is God's peace. Not the negative absence of conflict only, shalom is the positive presence of wholeness in our relationships with ourselves and others, God and nature. Christ died on the cross to bring about this wholeness because we cannot bring it about ourselves.

I remember how optimistic I felt about the world in the late fall of 1989 and winter of 1990. I stared in stunned yet ecstatic disbelief as I saw on television the Berlin wall being torn down. I listened attentively to reports of the collapse of one communist regime after another in Eastern Europe. When the Soviet Union crumbled, I felt free of the nagging fear of nuclear war that had plagued my generation since the Cold War began in the days following World War II.

But before I had time to savor our newfound optimism, it went sour. Saddam Hussein invaded Kuwait, sparking the death and destruction of the Gulf War. Violence against immigrants erupted in the new united Germany. A brutal civil war broke out in the former Yugoslavia. Gaunt and starving children stared out from the cover of *Time* magazine, victims of famine in Somalia.

Why does this always happen? Why does one oppression pass from the scene only to prepare the way for something worse? Why are hope and despair so intermingled in history? What accounts for this inability to end war and suffering once and for all? The Christian answer is that we live in a fallen world; our sin nature makes perfect peace impossible. T. S. Eliot expresses the tragedy of this fact in his play *Murder in the Cathedral:*

We are soiled by a filth that we cannot clean, united to supernatural vermin
It is not we alone, it is not the house, it is not the city that is defiled,

But the world that is wholly foul.[3]

One need not adopt Eliot's cynicism to agree that something is terribly wrong on Planet Earth. The inability of groups and nations to live at peace stems from the corruption of the human heart. Sin is the habit of making an idol of anything other than God, of turning inward in self-worship, whether subtly or blatantly. It is admitting with the apostle Paul, "I do not do the good I want, but the evil I do not want is what I do" (Romans 7:19).

Healing the Most Toxic Addiction of All

Sin is a power that we cannot break without God's help.

While writing this book, I had an experience that taught me this anew: My home was burglarized. At noon, while in a meeting at church, I received a call from a policeman who told me to come home immediately. When I got there, I found that my back door had been kicked in and my computer and printer, VCR, typewriter, and other electronic equipment had been stolen.

Fortunately for me, when my neighbor, a seventy-six-year-old grandmother, noticed three men loading these items into a car, she called 911. One of the three robbers peered through her kitchen window and saw her on the phone, however. He panicked and began breaking down her back door. Ready to do her harm, he was scared away by the approaching sirens. A high-speed chase ensued. The burglars drove their stolen car the wrong way down a busy city street for several miles, dodging vehicles and pedestrians. They eventually hit another vehicle and then fled on foot. They were found hiding in a nearby garage and were arrested at gunpoint.

After all the commotion caused by the television and newspaper coverage calmed down, my life began to return to normal. I recovered my property from the police and made arrangements to have the damage to my home repaired. Then, totally out of the blue, I received a letter from one of the thieves, written from the state prison. The letter arrived about a week after the break-in; it was from the youngest of the men, a twenty-six-year-old who had been imprisoned on three other occasions and had already served seven years. I was amazed to hear him apologize for causing me so much pain and tell why he had done it: He was so heavily under the influence of alcohol and drugs that he didn't know what he was doing.

Sin has this same lethal effect. To paraphrase J. Keith Miller, sin is the deadliest addiction of all. Under its influence, we live unconsciously. We turn our needs into greeds, give ourselves to unhealthy goals and relationships, and act in ways that hurt ourselves and others. When sin has power over us, it makes our lives miserable.[4]

Only grace can show us the way to freedom, and grace is the message of the cross. At Calvary, Jesus made atonement for our sin and the sin of the world. This *at-one-ment*, this intimate bonding of believers with God through the blood of Christ, brings perfect shalom, the wholeness of the soul forgiven and at peace.

But the bonding of believers with God through the Crucifixion requires the prior bonding of divinity with humanity in Christ's Incarnation. One ordinary human being dying for another would not bring about the at-one-ment with God for which we long. As an undergraduate at the University of Washington, I took a course on the history of Christianity during which a visiting lecturer made this point in a dramatic way. He walked on the students' desks from the back to the front of the room to get our attention. Then, outstretching his arms against the wall behind the professor's lectern, he cried out, "Crucify me! Crucify me!" His theatrics shocked us into realizing that unless Christ was God incarnate, the cross would have no more atoning value than you dying for me, or me for you. This is why the apostle Paul emphasized that "God was *in* Christ reconciling the world to himself" (2 Corinthians 5:19, RSV).

A God Big Enough to Take the Blame

The cross speaks of costly grace. Someone had to pay the price for humanity's sin. Otherwise all of history's wrongs would never be righted or its brokenness healed. The Christian message declares that we live on a visited planet: For a brief period of thirty-three years, God became one of us in Jesus of Nazareth. At the cross, God was in Christ, bearing the consequences of human evil, suffering and dying for all the wars ever fought, all the injustices ever committed, all the hate and violence and decadence ever known or imagined.

If the deity of Christ is not affirmed, Christianity cannot be Good News, only good advice. A Christ who is human but not also divine cannot reconcile us to God; he can only leave behind an example of goodness and a set of moral teachings for us to follow. But as fallen and fallible as we are, our following will be imperfect at best.

Nor can we divide the Trinity. In one understanding of the cross, it is suggested that God abandons Jesus, that the Creator remains in heaven, removed from the scene of suffering, while the Redeemer bears the full force of God's wrath and punishment for sin, alone. Upon hearing this explanation of the cross, a recent convert expressed his confusion by commenting, "I love Jesus, but I hate God."[5]

Donald Baillie wrote his book *God Was in Christ* to help people avoid these misunderstandings. He asks the same question raised by the fictional character Piers Plowman in the classic middle-English poem that bears his name: "Who suffers more than God?" Baillie's answer is, "No one." The statement "God was in Christ" suggests we cannot talk of a Christ who is only human and not divine. The meaning of the cross is that God bore the cost of humanity's sin. Christ's suffering was God's suffering. The Creator did not abandon the Redeemer. The atonement took place within the very heart of God; it all happened in love within the fullness of the Godhead.[6]

But if the cross means that God suffered *for* us in Christ, it also means that God suffers *with* us. No other religion offers me the assurance that in my darkest hours I am never alone. The cross declares that God endures the darkness with me, that when I hurt the most, God hurts the most. The cross is the place of intimate bonding between my pain and God's pain.

A powerful play entitled *The Sign of Jonah* dramatizes this point. Written in the late 1940s by a German minister named Guenter Rutenborn, the play raises the question of who really was to blame for the terrible atrocities of World War II. The characters on stage suggest the obvious culprits: Hitler and the Nazis were to blame, of course. But what about the bureaucrats and an indifferent public? Were they not also at fault? As the conversation continues, a man arises from the audience and comes to the stage. Interrupting the actors, he shouts, "You are being superficial. You are not taking this case back to its ultimate source. Do you want to know who is really to blame? I'll tell you. God is." After all, reasons the man, God made the world and entrusted it to ruthless people. Therefore God is ultimately responsible not only for the horror of the concentration camps but also for the suffering and death of war.

This idea stuns the actors on the stage. After they recover from their initial shock, they decide to have God tried in court. When the verdict is rendered, God is found guilty of the crime of creation, and the judge pronounces the sentence: "I hereby sentence God to have to come and live in this wretched world the way we humans have to." Gabriel, Michael, and Raphael, the three archangels, are sent to execute the sentence. As Gabriel leaves, he says, "When God serves this sentence, I'll see to it that he knows obscurity and shame. He'll be born in a barn, on the back side of nowhere, with a peasant girl for a mother. He'll experience the stigma of being a Jew in a Jew-hating world, and there will be suspicion of shame about the manner of his birth."

Michael also speaks harshly: "When God serves his sentence, I'm going to see to it that he experiences frustration and insecurity. He'll have no place to lay his head. No one, not even his family, will ever fully understand him. In the end, the very people he wanted to help will turn against him, and he will know the frustration of not having accomplished what he set out to do."

As Raphael departs, he is heard saying to himself, "When God serves this sentence, I'm going to see to it that he knows what it is like to suffer and to die. He will be falsely accused, illegally tried, cursed, spit upon, and tortured. And then he will die the long slow death of a common criminal."

After the archangels leave, the house lights are dimmed. In the silent darkness the audience realizes that God has already served this sentence.[7] In Christ, God came among us to live in this world of tears, to taste disappointment, to suffer, and to die. This is the meaning of the cross, the place of bonding between the human and the divine.

Freed in Order to Free

Reflecting on this meaning during Lent opens the heart to receive grace. One's awareness of being accepted by God in Christ deepens; a spiritual communion develops that comforts the disturbed and disturbs the comfortable. In this communion there is never boredom, but hope and joy, wonder and praise. Bonded intimately with Christ at the cross, we live beyond the numbing sameness of the ordinary. His passion becomes our passion. The courage and faith with which he met his greatest challenge inspires us to meet our challenges in a similar spirit. True, we often fail to follow his example. When facing problems with our health or finances, our career or relationships, we sometimes feel like quitting. But Calvary says he didn't quit. His commitment was total.

Reflecting on the cross during Lent makes me ask, What attitude do I bring to the daily responsibilities and major goals of my life? When I am fatigued and feeling inadequate for the task at hand, how do I respond? With resignation? With the fear and despair that leave me defeated and broken? Or do I face my challenges in the spirit of Jesus Christ, the spirit that accepted the cross and trusted God for the victory?

Jesus' example suggests that those who persevere prevail; it says there is nobility in fighting on against the odds, even when all hope seems gone. This fighting spirit does not lighten the weight of one's burdens; it broadens the shoulders that carry them. So strengthened, Christians manage their problems with poise and bring salt and light to the world. Knowing that Jesus gave himself for us, we give ourselves for others. Grace received becomes grace shared. To feed the hungry and shelter the homeless, to heal the sick and free the oppressed--this is the work to which the cross calls every Christian. It is work that must be done even when the obstacles seem many and the progress slow.

There is a Chinese legend about a grandfather who became frustrated by a hill near his home that blocked the beautiful light of the rising sun. Every morning he got up early and, taking his son and grandson with him, climbed to the top of the hill. There he picked up a small stone, walked back down the hill, and dropped the stone on the other side of a stream near his home.

Every day he repeated this peculiar ritual.

Finally the grandson became impatient and asked the old man, "Grandfather, why do we do this?"

He answered, "Because as long as we repeat this ritual every day, and you teach your children and grandchildren also to carry the pebbles, one day we will move this hill."

"But grandfather," said the boy. "You'll never see the hill moved."

"Yes," the old man nodded, "but I *know* that someday it will be moved."

That grandfather's perseverance in the face of an impossible challenge embodies the spirit of the cross. What seemed like a defeat for Jesus was actually the greatest triumph of love over hate, of mercy over judgment, that the world has ever known. It was a triumph because he was true to himself and faith and God until the end, making salvation possible for all. Whenever I think of his example, I remember that my struggles against my personal problems and the world's evils are not in vain. I remember that even in defeat love wins. Any expression of love, in life or death, is a victory.

Lent invites everyone to participate in this victory, to share its power right here and now. The power of the cross brings empty, searching hearts to God, their true home. Where there is guilt, the cross offers forgiveness; where there is restlessness, peace. As we go with Jesus to Calvary, we find meaning and renewal. To follow him there, refusing to turn back when the going gets hard, is to leave boredom behind. To follow him to the cross is to bond with him in death and begin the adventure of resurrection life.

Prayer for Palm/Passion Sunday

Shallow and inadequate is my love for you,
blessed Lord,
compared with
the heighth
and depth
and length
and breadth
of your love for me in Jesus Christ.

I encounter your love in many places,
   but never more powerfully than
   when I stand beneath his cross.

From the perspective of Calvary,
   I see you entering into
   the energy and fatigue,
      the challenge and crisis,
         the dignity and tragedy
   of the human struggle.

I draw near to you in prayer,
   seeking a deeper experience
   of your presence,
   that I might respond to all
   that your cross calls me to do and be.

Apart from you my life is empty,
   a chasing after the wind,
      a meaningless accumulation of years.

I need you, O God.

Not as a crutch,
   not as a panacea for my problems
   do I need you,
   but as the Source and Goal of all that I am.

You endured the cross to say you also need me,
   that your life, as mine, finds its highest
   fulfillment in bonding with another.

You came in Christ to be the world's liberating Savior
   and saving Liberator,
   a man of sorrows and acquainted with grief.

I do not look for another;
   I acknowledge you as Lord.

In turning to you in faith,
   I turn away from doubt and fear,
   from negativity and shame.

Thank you for washing me in the blood of the Lamb,
   for setting me free in Christ.

Confront me with the places in myself still in bondage,
    I pray.

I confess that,
    amid the pressures of the daily grind,
    I allow the demands of the moment to
    take priority over knowing you
    and making you known.

I come to you to reorient my thinking,
    that I might not be conformed to this world,
    but transformed by the renewing of my mind.

Though I can never be worthy of your gift of mercy,
    teach me to be thankful,
    and empower me so to live in attitude and action
    that my thanksgiving might be expressed,
    not only in word,
    but also in deed. Amen.

Questions for Reflection and Study

1. The point is made in this chapter that no entertainment is ever entertaining enough to keep people from eventually getting bored. If this is true, how is the cross of Jesus Christ relevant to solving the problem? What spiritual needs does Christian worship meet that entertainment doesn't? And what should be the relationship between Christ-centered worship and the universal human desire to be entertained?

2. Discuss the difference between Gabriel Fackre's definition of sin stated in this chapter and the idea of sin as "dos and don'ts." By any definition, does the concept of sin still have meaning in today's world? What can the church do to communicate the Christian message in a contemporary way?

3. Reflect on J. Keith Miller's description of sin as the deadliest addiction of all. What is the relationship between sin and addiction? Are the two synonymous, or is there more to the problem of being human than the tendency to fall into compulsive behaviors?

4. Why is the idea of atonement so essential to Christianity? What effect does the elimination of this idea have on the Christian message? What implications does this elimination have for the mission of the church?

5. Why is it important to keep the unity of the Trinity in mind when thinking about the meaning of the cross? Why is the concept of bonding, when applied to the relationships among the Persons of the Godhead, helpful yet inadequate in describing this unity?

6. What personal meaning or comfort do you find in the idea that God suffers with us, as well as for us, in Christ? How does this idea inform your response when, in Rabbi Harold Kushner's phrase, "bad things happen to good people"?

7. Was Jesus' choice to accept the cross simply a brave personal decision? Or was it meant to be a model for how his followers should respond to evil people and systems? What has the cross meant in your life?

8. What are some ways in which the cross was a triumph instead of a tragedy? Are there any lessons here about what a Christian's dominant life perspective and attitudes should be?

Notes

[1] *Wall Street Journal* (March 15, 1990), 1.

[2] Gabriel Fackre, *The Christian Story* (Grand Rapids: Eerdmans, 1978), 72.

[3] T. S. Eliot, *Murder in the Cathedral* (New York: Harcourt, Brace & World, Inc., 1935), 76-77.

[4] J. Keith Miller, *Hope in the Fast Lane* (New York: Harper Collins, 1991).

[5] Fackre, 120.

[6] D. M. Baillie, *God Was in Christ* (New York: Charles Scribner's Sons, 1948), 175, 188.

[7] See Bob Woods, "Christmas: The Light That Makes Us Human," *Pulpit Digest*, vol. LXV, no. 476 (November/December 1985), 60-61.

7

When Endings Become Beginnings

A Reading from the Gospel According to Matthew (28:1-10)
After the sabbath, as the first day of the week was dawning, Mary Magdalene and the other Mary went to see the tomb. And suddenly there was a great earthquake; for an angel of the Lord, descending from heaven, came and rolled back the stone and sat on it. His appearance was like lightning, and his clothing white as snow. For fear of him the guards shook and became like dead men. But the angel said to the women, "Do not be afraid; I know that you are looking for Jesus who was crucified. He is not here; for he has been raised, as he said. Come, see the place where he lay. Then go quickly and tell his disciples, 'He has been raised from the dead, and indeed he is going ahead of you to Galilee; there you will see him.' This is my message for you." So they left the tomb quickly with fear and great joy, and ran to tell his disciples. Suddenly Jesus met them and said, "Greetings!" And they came to him, took hold of his feet, and worshiped him. Then Jesus said to them, "Do not be afraid; go and tell my brothers to go to Galilee; there they will see me."

I always hate to see a good adventure end. The ending usually means a return to the ordinary, a rendezvous with business as usual. That's why joyous celebration erupts when what seems like an ending is actually a beginning.

Such an eruption occurs in C.S. Lewis's *Chronicles of Narnia,* one of the great adventure stories in Christian literature. Narnia is the enchanted land in which four children encounter dwarfs and nymphs, princes and witches. The children are befriended by Aslan, the gentle lion who represents Christ in Lewis's parable. Together with him they survive great dangers and fight ferocious battles; they even become kings and queens.

When the last adventure in Narnia concludes, the children fear that Aslan will send them back to the Shadowlands, the name used for the ordinariness of their home in England. But he surprises them. The ending turns out to be a beginning. When they and their parents die in an accident, Aslan declares, "The term is over: the holidays have begun. The dream is ended: this is the morning." Lewis then explains the children's passage from death to eternal life by saying, "Now at last they were beginning Chapter One of the Great Story, which no one on earth has read: which goes on for ever: in which every chapter is better than the one before."[1]

From Anguish to Alleluia

I have often come to the end of Lent with the same fear that the children had in Narnia. Seeing Jesus on the cross makes me afraid that the adventure of following him is over. The agony of Calvary raises many questions in my mind: Did his dream of the kingdom of God die with him? Were his actions on behalf of peace and justice all for naught? Should I still believe in radical love even when it got him crucified?

As Lent ends in the crucible of suffering and death, it staggers my spirit with an unsettling thought: If Jesus is dead for good, I am dead for good. Without him, I have no forgiveness for yesterday, no trustworthy values for today, no hope for tomorrow. My life becomes a wilderness, a barren desert of busyness and boredom. Realizing this, I grieve Jesus' death for his sake, but also for mine.

I wonder if that is also how his friends felt as they stood in the shadow of the cross. I suspect that they wept for him, but also for themselves. He had taken them beyond the ordinary, had led them on a great adventure toward the kingdom of God. But now it was over. Finished! They had no choice but to return to business as usual.

Most of the men did not stay with Jesus until the end. They ran away. I wonder if a return to their monotonous routine proved alluring amid the trauma and tragedy of Calvary. Long days of rigging the boats and tending the nets beckoned the two sets of brothers who were fishermen—Peter and Andrew, James and John. Perhaps Matthew prepared to go back to his tax collector's booth; maybe Simon made plans to resume his risky but predictable paramilitary career as a Zealot. I do not know. But of this I am sure: Any job would have seemed humdrum after being with Jesus.

He was as unconventional as he was revolutionary. Those who shared an intimate relationship with him found themselves reborn—positively changed! In his presence they never knew what was coming next, but because they had bonded with him, and he with them, they never got bored.

Then came the cross. It stopped the adventure of faith dead in its tracks. Even for the women, brave and true to the end, there was nothing left to do but try to give Jesus a proper burial. So they came to the tomb, early in the morning on the first day of the week, numb with grief, bearing spices with which to anoint his body.

What greeted them was the surprise of their lives. According to Matthew, ". . . there was a great earthquake; for an angel of the Lord, descending from heaven, came and rolled back the stone and sat upon it. His appearance was like lightning, and his clothing white as snow. For fear of him the guards shook and became like dead men" (Matthew 28:2-4). The angel's words to the women struck a note of hope, a resounding crescendo of triumph: "Do not be afraid; I know that you are looking for Jesus who was crucified. He is not here; for he has been raised, as he said. Come, see the place where he lay" (vv. 5-6).

Because of Easter, the tragedy of the cross was not final. The adventure of faith had not ended; it was only beginning. Now all people would be invited to share it, not just a few in Galilee. And who were the first to discover this? The women. Those who did not have the right to bear witness in the Jewish courts became the first to proclaim the Resurrection. No one would have given them this privilege unless Easter really happened. Men would have been cast in the lead roles if someone were making it all up, because men were the only ones who would have been believed.

Having seen the tomb empty, and having heard the angel's message, the women ran "with fear and great joy" to tell the disciples. They were entering a new dimension of life, moving to a higher level of bonding, not with the dead Jesus but with the risen and victorious Christ. There are three reasons why this bonding is life's most transforming experience: Easter is power; Easter is promise; Easter is purpose.[2] Those who integrate these affirmations into their hearts will join the women in the supreme adventure of resurrection living.

Easter Is Power

Have you ever stopped to ask what humanity's greatest enemy is? I do not believe it is any oppressive disease or political system, any tenacious economic problem or social injustice, as brutal as these are. Humanity's greatest enemy is death. Death defies human control and understanding. It dissolves bonds of love, strikes with calloused disregard for circumstances, and threatens to render life and goodness meaningless.

No wonder death has been called "the Grim Reaper": There is no escaping it, no matter how far or fast one runs. Ingenious methods have been used to slow the aging process, to hold death at bay, but all eventually fail. In the late 1980s, the mother of a teenager named Ryan White had to tell her hemophiliac son that he had been diagnosed with AIDS. (He would later become a national symbol of the struggle against the disease.) She waited until the family's Christmas celebrations were over, then shared with him what the doctors had told her. After hearing the tragic diagnosis, Ryan asked her, "Does this mean I'm going to die?"

"Yes," she said, "it does. *But we are all going to die sometime.*"

Without Easter, what hope do we have in the face of such a certain destiny? Only human hope. But I need more than that. All of my personal resources fail me in death's presence; I need a power greater than my own to help me stand. Easter makes that power available.

The resurrection of Christ means that evil and death have been defeated. If Christ was God in human flesh and we killed him, the Crucifixion was the most heinous crime in history. As Christ lay in the tomb on the night of Good Friday through the sabbath on Saturday, it seemed that hate had triumphed over love. Cruelty, it seemed, had dealt compassion a fatal blow, and darkness had extinguished all light.

But God did not allow the agony and injustice of the cross to have the last word. By raising Christ from the dead, God declared love and life and light victorious over all their foes. In the words of the distinguished New Testament scholar Amos Wilder:

> Retell, renew the event
> In these planetary years,
> For we were there and He is here:
> It is always the third day.[3]

It is always the third day! Wasn't that the essence of the angel's message at the empty tomb? The angel wanted the women to know that the anguish of Friday and the gloom of Saturday had passed. If God has defeated death, the third day is forever!

True, we still live in a Good Friday world, where unfairness and suffering abound. But now death's sting is gone. The power of God has prevailed. As theologian Gabriel Fackre says, "The cross was the weapon of suffering love, persuasion not coercion, that befits the God who will not act contrary to the divine nature. The sign that this weapon *does* defeat the dark powers is the resurrection."[4]

Christians now share the third day's victory. Knowing that death itself has died frees one from fear of the future. Believing one is destined for a homecoming, not a defeat, at the end of life, lets one begin living to the fullest right now. This fullness is Easter's gift. The gift comes from the same power that raised Christ from the dead. But although this power is available to all believers, it must be received by faith and integrated into one's life.

Easter's power is like electricity before it was harnessed, like nuclear energy before the atom was split. It is a present power with unlimited potential for good, but it must be discovered before it can be used. The women at the empty tomb modeled the only method of discovery that works: They bonded with the risen Christ. What they thought was an ending became a beginning when they surrendered fully to him, renewing their adventure of faith.

The power of a new beginning is at the heart of the Christian faith. Christ demonstrated this power. His life ended on the cross, but his physical body was raised and transfigured into a "spiritual body." His Easter appearances were not merely psychic events in the lives of those who saw him. Nor was Easter simply a resurgence of faith on the part of his followers. Easter was the power of God creating something new and alive and glorious out of something old and dead and ordinary.[5]

As Christ was changed from a physical presence to a spiritual one, so can our weaknesses become strengths through his energizing work within us. Easter is the power to turn shame to dignity, despair to hope. Consider the disciples. Many of them acted in a cowardly manner when Jesus needed them most. His crucifixion left them broken and despondent. But Easter transformed them. The same Simon Peter who denied Christ three times and hid with the others in the upper room, utterly dejected, later preached heroically. The same James who, throughout the Gospels, is portrayed as a brother of Jesus who did not believe in him became the leader of the Jerusalem church after the Resurrection. And the same Saul of Tarsus, a fanatical persecutor of Christians, met the risen Lord on the Damascus road and became Paul the apostle.

Why were these new beginnings possible? Because Easter is power. Because Easter proclaims that the way things are need not be the way they stay. Christians have access to what Thomas Chalmers, in his famous nineteenth-century sermon (mentioned in chapter one), called "The Expulsive Power of a New Affection." Chalmers's point was that our destructive attitudes and habits are like the few dead leaves that cling to a tree's branches all winter long rather than falling to the ground in autumn. These vestiges of deadness are only discarded when the sap rises in the spring and replaces them with new leaves.

So it is with resurrection life. Bonding with the risen Christ avails one of an unfailing inner resource. This spiritual power dispels fear and negativity and despair. Life looks brighter than ever before, not because it has changed but because *you* have changed. No longer trapped in the cycle of haste without direction that breeds exhaustion without satisfaction, you begin an adventure beyond the ordinary—and never turn back.

Easter Is Promise

The only power worth its salt is the kind that accomplishes good. Easter's power accomplishes God's will. When Christ died on the cross, it seemed his ideals died with him. But Easter says those ideals are eternal, that they came from the very heart of God. Easter is the promise that it is right to love one's enemies, to forgive those who hurt you, to lay up treasures in heaven and not on earth. Easter vindicates Jesus' teachings about feeding the hungry and healing the sick, about clothing the naked and freeing the oppressed. Easter is the promise that one day all humanity will acknowledge these teachings as truth.

That day will come at the end of time, at the consummation of all things. In the words of German theologian Jürgen Moltmann, "Anyone who sees the risen Christ is looking in advance into the coming glory of God. He perceives something which is not otherwise perceptible, but which will one day be perceived by everyone."[6]

When I become discouraged about the state of the world, Easter reminds me that tragedy and tyranny are not forever. Their part in history's drama has entered its last act, with God's hand ready to draw the final curtain. Or, to use the metaphor suggested by Professor Gordon Fee, Easter can be compared with V-E Day, and the consummation with V-J Day. On May 8, 1945—V-E Day—the European phase of World War II ended with Germany's surrender to the Allied Forces. The war continued, however, until August 15, 1945—V-J Day—when Japan was finally defeated and all fighting ended.

We now live in an interim period. Sin and death were defeated in "portent and principle"[7] at the cross and empty tomb but will be conquered finally when, in the words of Revelation, "The kingdom of this world has become the kingdom of our Lord and of his Messiah, and he will reign forever and ever" (Revelation 11:15). Easter's promise is hope; it is the promise that, no matter what happens on earth, God is still in control and one day will bring to fulfillment all that Christ came to do and teach.

History is moving toward a climax. A glorious triumph of good over evil, of God's light over the world's darkness, awaits. If this were not so, we would have no alternative but to submit to despair in the face of death's inevitability. Ernest Becker would be right: "The soberest conclusion that we could make about what has actually been taking place on the planet for about three billion years is that it is being turned into a vast pit of fertilizer."[8] The angel's words to the women mean this is not true. The world belongs to God; God will never abandon us. That is Easter's promise. Through the worst that can happen, even through death itself, God stays with us forever.

The promise applies to all of life. Easter's hope lifts tired but believing spirits when they struggle. It is hope for fragmented relationships, for shattered dreams, for broken lives. It even inspires people to attempt the impossible. Many of us must make this attempt whether we want to or not. Overcoming a handicap, battling an addiction, coping with declining health, handling a family crisis, even getting an education or searching for a new job—these sometimes seem like impossible challenges.

But the Easter promise of new life in Christ invigorates our spirits. It brings us to that place of absolute commitment, of unshakable confidence, which is necessary for us to prevail. It keeps us fighting on against all odds, refusing to quit when the going gets tough, coming back after each discouragement and defeat more determined than ever to succeed. Easter enables us to make the motto of the Special Olympics our own: "Let me win. But if I cannot win, let me be brave in the attempt."

In his book *The Unexpected Universe,* Loren Eiseley tells of walking the beach in Costabel. Struck by how the tidal plain was littered with the dying debris of sea life, he felt special sympathy for the starfish, their breathing spores stuffed with sand, who could not fight their way back to the water because the surf would cast them repeatedly back upon the shore. Amid this scene of death and despair, Eiseley came upon a man who was a star-thrower. The man walked the beach picking up the dying starfish and, one after another, tossed them as far as he could out to the sea. Eiseley watched him for a time, fascinated by his effort to give hope to the dying. Then he joined him. Later, having pondered the meaning of it all, he wrote, "Somewhere. . . there is a hurler of stars, and he walks, because he chooses, always in desolation, but not in defeat."⁹

The risen Christ is a star-thrower. Having conquered death and despair himself, his mission is to help others do the same. Bonding with him enables one to meet life's challenges with confidence and resilience. Each day becomes an opportunity to transcend one's limits, and that means no more boredom. Instead, the promise of his presence brings renewal to the dullest routine.

Easter Is Purpose

Assured of death's defeat, people have a reason to live. The hope of resurrection dispels futility. Knowing that the grave is not our final destiny, we find meaning here and now. We are no longer afraid that our time in this world is "a tale told by an idiot, full of sound and fury, signifying nothing."

Easter helps me not to be intimidated by a conversation Don Quixote had with Sancho Panza in the movie *Man of La Mancha.* Quixote is reminiscing about the soldiers who have died in his arms. In remembering their agony, he recalls feeling that they wanted him to answer a haunting question. Sancho asks, "Was it the question 'Why am I dying?' "No," Quixote replies, "it was the question 'Why was I living?' "

Many people in the 1990s have no satisfying answer to this question. Some find themselves trapped in careers or marriages or religious understandings that once made sense but no longer do. Others have ridden their talents into the glittering skies of material success, only to ask, Is this all there is? Still others are plagued by self-doubt after tasting failure or defeat. Carl Jung spoke of these hurting people in *Modern Man in Search of a Soul,* where he said, "About a third of my cases are suffering from no clinically definable neurosis, but from the senselessness and emptiness of their lives."¹⁰

Easter offers an answer because it infuses life with purpose. If I believe that death is not as much an ending as a beginning, I incorporate the positive spirit of that affirmation into my goals and relationships, my attitudes and lifestyle. The gratitude I feel over the victory of the Resurrection spills over into my outlook on life. I refuse to be cynical about today because the empty tomb reminds me of the new tomorrow God is preparing. In the light of Easter, my purpose is no longer limited to this world; I live in the here and now as a citizen of the there and then. Bearing witness to the kingdom of God, as Jesus did, becomes my passion.

The women found this renewed sense of purpose as they ran to tell the disciples what they had seen and heard. Jesus met them and said, "Greetings!" Then they "took hold of his feet, and worshiped him" (Matthew 28:9). The Easter miracle inspired this spiritual encounter. It lifted the women out of their lethargy and gave them something to live for. They no longer belonged to themselves but to their crucified and risen Lord. Knowing him and making him known became their passion; it filled their hearts with joy.

Abby Hirsch, president of the Emotional Trends Institute in New York, did research on the lives of modern women. Her findings evoke thoughts of the women of Easter. According to Hirsch, many women would prefer to go "hand-to-mouth than 9-to-5." This is because adventure—climbing a mountain, going down rivers, working at a challenging job—helps one feel "connected to one's life."[11]

I suspect that "connected" is how the women felt as they met the risen Christ. Renewed in faith, they shared a deepened communion with him. This communion restored the purpose of their lives. Call it self-knowledge. Call it spiritual freedom or mystical union. I call this communion bonding with the risen Lord, an experience that banishes boredom and opens new possibilities for growth.

A person who has bonded with Christ begins looking for ways to bring his love to the world. This person is freed from the endless struggle to keep entertained. Rather than being a daily grind governed by the elusive goal of personal fulfillment, life becomes a celebration of sharing. Meaning is found when one finds one's mission.

Bored with their successful law practice and affluent lifestyle, Millard and Linda Fuller decided to give it all up. They sold their possessions and joined Clarence Jordan at a Christian community called Koinonia Farms in Americus, Georgia. Their mission eventually became Habitat for Humanity, a worldwide movement they founded to provide decent housing for all people everywhere. Initially the Fullers simply wanted to eliminate substandard housing in Sumter County, Georgia (population twenty-seven thousand). But in less than two decades Habitat for Humanity has spread to hundreds of cities in the United States, several Canadian provinces, and more than twenty-five other countries. "We invited the whole world to an adventure for God," says Millard Fuller, "an adventure that would bring all the churches together."[12]

Seen from the perspective of Easter, all of life is "an adventure for God." The wonder of this adventure is that it may even continue beyond the grave. Jesus suggested this idea in his words, "In my Father's house are many mansions" (John 14:2, KJV). What could this mean? Is not a mansion a house in and of itself? The Greek word translated "mansion" is *monai*, about which there is much debate. Some scholars think *monai* means an abiding-place, a place where a person remains. But I am intrigued by the suggestion of Archbishop William Temple that "the resting-places are wayside *caravanserais*—shelters at stages along the road where travellers may rest on their journey."[13]

Was Jesus saying that spiritual growth continues beyond death? that there are resting-places provided as one progresses on the adventure toward complete bonding with God? This is Leslie D. Weatherhead's conclusion in one of his London City Temple sermons. He describes these resting-places as "inns of increasing happiness, of deeper and deeper communion with God, of clearer and clearer understanding . . . , until at last we become all that God can make us and are united with Him for ever. This final dwelling-place . . . is called by the saints and mystics 'the beatific vision.' "[14]

Christians long to see this vision. More wonderful than words can tell, more glorious than minds can imagine, the vision awaits all who journey with Christ beyond death into life eternal. I am thankful that Lent invites us into this deep spiritual communion, and that the power, promise, and purpose of Easter make the invitation possible.

In the days ahead I want to continue seeking the beatific vision, and I hope you do, too. Easter may mark the end of the Lenten season, but the search for the vision is not over; it has only begun. Having shared the experiences of the people we have met in this study, I feel strengthened to go on. True, the life of faith won't be any easier for us than it was for them; there will be many trials in the wilderness along the way, and boredom's curse will always be with us, no matter what methods we use to try to overcome it.

But the curse will not have the last word. Its power is broken when we form the same spiritual bond with Jesus that he formed with God. Because Lent gives us the opportunity to solidify this bond, it is more than a season; it's a journey from sacrifice to celebration. To take this journey is to transcend the daily grind and find a new and extraordinary life. It is to rejoice in the message of Easter: Christ is risen! Alleluia!

Prayer for Easter Sunday

Almighty God,
>by whose power tragedy becomes triumph,
>I seek you not among the dead
>but among the living.

I rejoice today because
>the tomb is empty,
>>the stone rolled away,
>>>the Easter miracle accomplished.

When I thought the adventure of following Christ was over,
>you surprised me with the good news
>that it was just beginning.

You did not leave me without hope;
>you fought the battle against death and despair
>until the victory was won.

Now I need not be afraid.

No matter how dark the night,
>no matter how hard the struggle or ominous the foe,
>>I am more than a conqueror
>>through him who loved me.

Thank you, Lord, for proving that
>nothing is impossible for you,

for kindling the fires
of resurrection and renewal
in the ashes of defeat.

I want to be a pilgrim on the resurrection road,
    the same road that the women walked
on their way to an encounter
with the risen Christ.

I confess that my steps are often tentative, O God.

Other distractions keep me from beginning the journey.

I prefer to walk easier roads,
    roads that lead to
        worldly recognition,
        material gain,
           personal comfort.

On this Easter day,
    remind me of the surpassing
worth of knowing Christ Jesus my Lord,
of encountering him at the empty tomb.

I surrender to you everything that is dead within me—
    my stillborn dreams,
        my unhealed wounds,
           my besetting anxieties.

O God of new beginnings,
    bring life where there is death,
    I pray.

Set before me some high challenge
    that will force me to rely on your power,
    the power at work within me to do far more
    abundantly than all I can ask or imagine.

Focus my thoughts not on what I cannot do
    because of my limitations,
    but on what you want to do
    in and through me by your Spirit.

May I live in the light of Easter's dawn,

and may there always be room
for an alleluia in my heart. Amen.

Questions for Reflection and Study

1. Read 1 Corinthians 13:12 and reflect on C. S. Lewis's description of life in this world as the "Shadowlands." Does this image ring true for you? If so, how does it influence your feeling about death? When is death a friend rather than an enemy?

2. Contrast the roles of the women and the men in the Easter story. What conclusions, if any, can be drawn from the fact that the women are featured so prominently?

3. In the view of some, the bodily resurrection of Christ is not an essential Christian belief. Do you agree or disagree? If the orthodox teaching about the Resurrection is denied, what implications does this have for how Christians are to think about the body in this life and beyond? Refer to 1 Corinthians 15:35-58 in responding.

4. What explanation can you give for the change that occurred in the disciples' lives after Easter? Are there lessons for today that can be drawn from their spiritual biographies?

5. What is the relationship between the Resurrection and the ethics of Jesus, as set forth in the Sermon on the Mount? What about the link between the Resurrection and the end of history?

6. How can the Resurrection be a source of inspiration in the struggle for social justice or personal wholeness?

7. Is there any difference between bonding with the human Jesus and bonding with the risen Lord? What are some of the limitations placed on the Christian life if one believes in Jesus as only a great moral teacher and not the Son of God?

8. Elisabeth Kübler-Ross has written a book entitled *Death: The Final Stage of Growth*. But is death really where growth ends? Compare Kübler-Ross's perspective with the one articulated by Leslie Weatherhead at the end of this chapter.

Notes

[1] C. S. Lewis, *The Last Battle* (New York: Collier Books, 1973), 184.

[2] I express gratitude to Lewis B. Smedes, whose chapter on grace in his book *How Can It Be All Right When Everything Is All Wrong?* (New York: Harper & Row, 1982) inspired the first two points of this outline.

[3] Amos Niven Wilder, "The Third Day," *Grace Confounding* (Philadelphia: Fortress Press, 1972), 3.

[4] Gabriel Fackre, *The Christian Story* (Grand Rapids: Eerdmans, 1978), 123.

[5] Fackre, 140.

[6] Jürgen Moltmann, *The Trinity and the Kingdom* (San Francisco: Harper San Francisco, 1981), 85.

[7] Ibid., 141.

[8] Ernest Becker, *The Denial of Death* (New York: The Free Press, 1973), 283.

[9] Loren Eiseley, *The Unexpected Universe* (New York: Harcourt, Brace & World, 1969), 69-91.

[10] Quoted in Harold S. Kushner, *When All You've Ever Wanted Isn't Enough* (New York: Summit Books, 1986), 18.

[11] Quoted on the "Sally Jessy Raphael Show," September 10, 1992 (see transcript no. 1049, 5-6).

[12] Quoted in William H. Willimon, "Millard Fuller's Theology of the Hammer," *Christian Century* (October 5, 1988), 862-863.

[13] Quoted in Leslie D. Weatherhead, *Key Next Door* (Nashville: Abingdon Press, 1959), 248.

[14] Ibid., 249.